At the beginning of this year I submitted to be photo'ed, at last—for many nieces, and a few old friends. I must think that you are an old friend as well as a very kind and constant one; and so I don't like not to send you what I have sent others. The artist who took me (as he always does) three several views of one's face; but the third view, looking full face, got blurred by my blinking at the light; so only these two were reproduced—I should not know that either was meant for (me) nor, I think, would anyone else, if not told; but the truth-telling sun somehow did them; as he acted so handsomely by me, I took courage to distribute them to those who have a regard for me, and will naturally like to have so favourable a version of one's outward aspect to remember one by. I should not have sent them had it been otherwise. The up looking one I call "The Statesman" quite ready to be called to the helm of affairs: the down looking one I call the philosopher. Will you take which one you like? and when old Spedding comes your way give him the other (he won't care which) with my love.

LETTER DATED MARCH 30, 1873, WRITTEN BY EDWARD FITZ-GERALD TO SIR FREDERICK POLLOCK, ON THE SUBJECT OF BEING PHOTOGRAPHED. FROM "THE SPHERE," ISSUE OF MARCH 27, 1909, WHICH CARRIED AN ARTICLE BY JOHN LODER (FITZGERALD'S BOOKSELLER) ON THE FITZGERALD CENTENARY.

Into an Old Room

EDWARD FITZGERALD

ALSO BY PETER DE POLNAY

~~~~~~

Two Mirrors

The Umbrella Thorn

The Moot Point

~~~~~~

CREATIVE AGE PRESS, INC., NEW YORK

PETER DE POLNAY

Into an Old Room

A MEMOIR OF EDWARD FITZGERALD

CREATIVE AGE PRESS, INC., NEW YORK

55

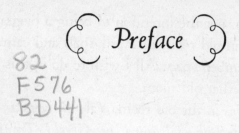

Preface

"BOULGE," said Edward FitzGerald of his family's permanent and my temporary home, "is one of the ugliest places in England—one of the dullest—" and, as a punishment, his biographers, with the exception of A. C. Benson in his *Edward FitzGerald* (English Men of Letters Series; Macmillan, 1905), have written dull lives of him, making him seem dull, too, and spinsterish, like the pollard oaks of Boulge. Admittedly it is a difficult task to approach an eminent Victorian. He is covered with a shroud of respectability and nothing peeps out. Yet during my stay at Boulge, next door to his grave, I felt him signaling with all his eccentricity, originality, genius, and greatness: signaling madly from underneath the shroud. And the trees, the Suffolk wind, and the wild flowers called out for him.

But let it be said at once that this book has neither

the pretension nor the intention of being a biography. I went into an old room in April 1946 and came out of it in September 1947. All I wish to do in this book is to describe that old room.

While I was in the old room, Yale University Press published *The Life of Edward FitzGerald, Translator of The Rubáiyát of Omar Khayyám,* by Alfred McKinley Terhune. Mr. Terhune went to the same sources as I, namely to the library of Trinity College, Cambridge, where most of FitzGerald's published and unpublished letters are. When I read Mr. Terhune's book, I was glad to see that the unpublished letters I made use of are, generally speaking, not the letters Mr. Terhune fancied. Moreover, his FitzGerald is altogether different from the FitzGerald I came to know. The fact that a letter is unpublished does not *eo ipso* turn it into a better letter than a published one. Therefore it suited my purpose to use letters, published or not, as long as such letters fell in with the vague plan of this book. On the other hand, I found that Mr. Terhune went to the same sources as I for the Persian, but that is understandable since, I suppose, his acquaintance with Persian is as slight as mine. The sources I have mostly in mind are Edward G. Browne's *A Literary History of Persia* (Fisher Unwin, 1906), and Edward Heron-Allen's *Edward FitzGerald's Rubáiyát of Omar Khayyám* (Bernard Quaritch,

1899). For both these books, and for so many others, I am indebted to the help and advice of the Librarian of the London Library and his excellent staff.

Now that I am speeding toward the end of this preface, I had better thank everybody who helped and advised me in the seventeen months during which I collected the material for this book. I must thank Messrs. Macmillan & Co., for their permission to make use of the published letters and works of Fitz-Gerald; the Master and Fellows of Trinity College, Cambridge, for permission to make use of the unpublished material of and concerning FitzGerald at Trinity College Library; the Librarian and his assistants for their help and advice; the Librarian of Ipswich Public Library; Mr. C. Charles Paine, for providing me with copies of three letters of FitzGerald; Miss M. Cowper Smith, Bodham Donne's granddaughter, for putting at my disposal letters of FitzGerald and Fanny Kemble; the Rev. Father Eustace Clare, Chaplain of St. Joseph's College, Ipswich, and secretary of the Irish Genealogical Society, for helping me with the Irish background; Mr. W. G. Arnott of Woodbridge for the sale catalogue of Little Grange; Mr. Mewburn Levien; Messrs. G. Gaunt and T. W. Earp for many useful hints; and Mr. Roger Senhouse, who not only helped me continuously but understood my intentions even before I thought of them.

FitzGerald had many friends and many of these were distinguished men. It suited his biographers, when not too busy with him, to perambulate among them. However, I decided not to lay too much stress on his friends. They come into this book only if and when I require their presence, which is only when I need their help to make me understand better Fitz-Gerald's thoughts, moods, or actions.

Before leaving the preface behind, I had better describe a scene which explains the dedication. It is early October and the sun shines on the Backs of Cambridge. It is warm and pleasant outside. I am sitting on a hard stool in Wren's beautiful Trinity Library. In front of me are letters from FitzGerald, Tennyson, Carlyle, Spedding, and many more. I feel fidgety, for I want to go out and smoke a cigarette.

"I think," I say to my wife who sits beside me, "you ought to make a copy of this letter. I simply must go out and have a cigarette."

That happened often; those October days near the Cam were splendid, but mostly for me. Therefore, in true gratitude, I dedicate this book to my wife Margaret, and I should add that FitzGerald's handwriting is difficult to read, especially when the sun plays with the Cam.

Contents

Part One

Into an Old Room

~~~~~~

It is a wonderful thing that the written word, how-were breathing heavily as if they had asthma. They never spoke in my dream—truly they were just a conversation piece—and when I awoke I wondered, not without fear, whether their appearing in my dream would become a habit. John lay in the family vault with the entire family, Edward, as befits genius, next to it; so they were both near, and a short walk to the Hall could not upset even heavily breathing men.

But I never saw them again. When for months on end my thoughts were firmly clutching FitzGerald, there would have been an excuse if I had dreamt of him. Still I saw him only that once. On the last night, however, of my stay at Boulge, when the corridors were again resounding with my footsteps and the books again were stacked on the bare floor of the library, I awoke with a feeling akin to panic. The door rattled, but doors banged and rattled a lot at Boulge. I often called it the house of the banging doors. Yet as it rattled I was afraid, for my guilt was now greater. I had pried on him, I had listened at the keyhole, and I had, worst of all, begun a book about him. I switched on the light and I should not have been surprised had he come in "like a bear," as Thackeray said of him. Of course nobody came in till the removal men arrived next day.

But to return to the first night. When I awoke and could still see the brothers FitzGerald (Peter, the third brother, the kind and good Catholic, married to his cook, was as self-effacing in my dream as he had been in life), I said to myself I would not forget the boots, the laces, and tweeds—in fact, the Victorian paraphernalia of the Victorian brothers. For Edward FitzGerald's life wound and plowed its way through Victorian England. However much he was detached from his age and any other age, it remained materially his age. The air he breathed was the air the Queen breathed too, air that was thick with the smoke of ever-rising factory chimneys. There are men who are the makers of their age, others are made by their age, and others again slink through their times shivering and unhappy. FitzGerald was like none of them. Yet, his shawl and boa notwithstanding, he had to wear the costume of his age. So in that respect my dream was not entirely uninteresting.

As for the heavy breathing, the Rev. Mr. Doughty, late vicar of Martlesham, who was then gaily approaching the age of ninety (in Suffolk one lives a very long time), had told me a few days before that as a boy his father had taken him to an exhibition of painting in Ipswich and there he saw John and Edward. They had seemed huge men to his young eyes, and they both breathed stentoriously. They were, he thought, awe-inspiring. They were the same in my dream.

The Victorian background of FitzGerald's life was

5

with me the next day while carpets were laid down, books disentangled, and I slowly began to find my way about the house.

He was born in 1809 and died in 1883. The Queen came to the throne at the time he was peeling off his youth. But he had never been young.

Through middle age, throughout his creative years, the royal weeds floated before him and his friends. Some of his friends, like Tennyson and Carlyle, were, so to speak, incorporated in the Queen's system. How far, then, did all that influence him?

As I put the question my answer was already formulated, namely, that for the moment there was no answer. It is difficult to draw conclusions even from the living. Go for a long walk with your best friend, and suddenly, after a friendly silence during which you had imagined his thoughts in harmony with yours, he will say something that will leave you surprised, even stupefied, for you become aware that his thoughts and way of thinking are utterly hidden from you. It is more so with the dead: their silence is their wisecrack. Wrapped in silence, they do not answer back. One can hang any theories on the backs of the dead: they do not notice them.

When FitzGerald was a little boy of six, the tumbrils full of the wounded of Waterloo rattled through Wickham Market. When the Queen was crowned on

June 28, 1837, he was at Kitlands, near Leith Hill, with his friends James Spedding and W. F. Pollock as the guests of a Trinity tutor, Douglas Heath. In the grounds there was what one of his biographers, Thomas Wright, described as "an open bath." At the sound of the distant cannon they jumped into the water, and swam around singing "God Save the Queen." But that only shows that FitzGerald had good lungs, since it is not easy to swim and sing loyally at the same time.

When FitzGerald died, in 1883, the Queen still had many years to go, but the era of Victorian prosperity had already reached its peak, in fact had settled down on it. His own lifetime coincided with two distinct swings of the pendulum. From the end of the Napoleonic wars till the Crimean it swung to depression, fear of revolution, and dark skies; after the Crimean, notwithstanding that the Crimean produced for the first time in England a sense of the horrors and losses of wars, it swung to success, rewards of work, conquest, and more work. Yet somehow these two distinct ages seemed to have left FitzGerald equally unmoved.

It is a difficult task to try to define an age through the eyes of its contemporaries. A later generation finds it easy to sum up the Victorian age, to define and make partitions; for its contemporaries to do so is a little like passing final judgment on a play in the middle of the second act. Few people are ever satisfied with their own times. Saint-Simon had little good to say of the golden age of Louis XIV; Thackeray, Fitz-Gerald's friend, the man who in our eyes had a full share of the enviable well-being and well-doing of the Victorian age, wrote in March 1856 from America, ". . . after your time & mine after Englands perhaps in ½ a dozen generations when this the Great Empire of the world numbers 120 millions of citizens (and *esses*) at least when our old Europe is worn out, who knows whether the Great Republic may not colonise with its negroes the vacant British Isles?" *

Thus there was the smug Victorian, the successful novelist, who in the golden age of complete security was not loath to imagine his rich country, peopled with belching factory chimneys, as some day a desert land waiting for a new, though darker, race of men to give it life again, and to become, to quote the same letter when describing his journey to the Mississippi, a place where there are,

dirty meals, knives down everybody's throat, dirty bucks straddling over the balconies, their dirty boots as high as their heads . . . not one pretty aspect of nature for those hun-

* This quotation, as so many others which deal with Thackeray in this book, comes from that, for me, invaluable gold mine, *The Letters and Private Papers of William Makepeace Thackeray*, Collected and Edited by Gordon N. Ray.

dreds of miles except now and then a melancholy ragged vista of pines or live oaks fringed with a dreary funereal moss —nothing picturesque in the so called cities—only great straight streets of tenements chiefly wood—pigs cows and negroes sauntering about. . . .

Of course Thackeray was depicting his journey from Virginia to the Mississippi, but that was surely the picture he had in mind when he saw England populated by colored men.

Despair, needless to say, belongs to all ages, and the Victorians could well afford to indulge in it. FitzGerald despaired too of England. Things were bad, the end was in sight, England was sinking. In his case, however, it meant that he would love England more and more. He could love more deeply when he thought that all was lost and calamity was coming.

The Victorian in many respects is beyond our imagination, for he had an appetite which we in our restricted age hardly understand. There was appetite for work, for love, for books, for learning, for research, for exploration, for faith, for decency, for huge helpings of rich food, and for gushing tears. Now Fitz-Gerald, who has been labeled an Unvictorian Victorian, shared the appetite of his contemporaries. His reading was stupendous, especially if one bears in mind that anything he read once he read again; many books he read four or five times. His appetite to know and understand as much as possible of his native Suffolk was in the best tradition of his day. His appetite for love and tears was outstanding even for his time. Indeed, the heavy Victorian of the dream of my first night at Boulge Hall nearly fits—but not quite. For Fitz-Gerald had no appetite for lucre. Moreover, he was apart from and above his age because he was an individualist in every respect; that is to say, he was independent in mind and spirit. If one is independent in mind and spirit, one is either a revolutionary or an eccentric. FitzGerald chose to be an eccentric and his was an age which permitted eccentricity. All his adult life he was financially independent and it is a great point in favor of his age that it did not interfere with that independence. If it had, there would have been no Rubáiyát. The fact that an age allows a man to stand apart is a compliment to that age; and taking it all in all, not many ages nor many countries permitted that, either by custom or by habit. Pushkin, for example, could not stand aside but had to get himself killed in a duel.

It can, therefore, be said that FitzGerald could lead an Unvictorian existence thanks to the Victorian era. In FitzGerald's time England was not static (no age is), yet with wars, Corn Laws, Reform Bills, Irish troubles, etc., he was left undisturbed among his books, thoughts, friendships, and refined solitude. Only once did he take interest in an election and that was because he disliked one of the candidates.

Next in importance to a man's age come his background and early surroundings. In FitzGerald's case these were completely contradictory, a fact which must have helped a good deal in forming his character. Contradictory they were because he was of Irish origin yet had a Suffolk background. The cold winds of Suffolk driving the empty hard blue sky, blowing inland the anger of the German Ocean, die long before they cross into Essex; and Ireland, though a Suffolk man would care neither one way nor the other, is even further afield. The Irish belong to the entire world, whatever the world may think of them, but the Suffolk people are certain of two facts: that there is the sea on one side and some vague uncharted land on the other. There is Norfolk too, but only just. In the old days when Suffolk produced its fair share of gallows birds for Holborn Hill, though of course it was a one-way traffic, the people of Suffolk knew almost more of the outside world than in FitzGerald's time, or in ours; and then and yesterday and today the Irish were all over the place. Thus, to let his eye roam as far as the little tree near the hedge and yet to see the minarets of Khorassan had been granted to FitzGerald, thanks to his origin and background. But the background often triumphed over the origin, which was one of the reasons why he stayed with the little tree and cared not to know the minarets.

It was through the background that I found the origin. In Ipswich there is a narrow street, one of many narrow streets, and it is called Silent Street. At Number Three is a bookshop, the College Gateway bookshop. It belongs to Mr. Cook, with whom I have had many friendly hagglings. As Mr. Cook was the better man, he was invariably the winner, and thus I remain indebted to him for a number of books on Suffolk and FitzGerald.

On the left as one enters is a desk crowded with old numbers of Household Novels, Christian Novels, old film magazines, and the year before last's *Woman's Illustrated,* but the film magazines predominate. Mr. Cook used to tell me that, before his time and as far back as FitzGerald's time, this particular counter was laden with cheap editions of Dickens and Thackeray. It was a counter for servant girls and working girls, and it did a brisk trade. Today it has only film magazines and their like.

"Provided," said Mr. Cook, "they read, which is very rare. Most of them never read at all, they just go to the cinema." One more mark for the Victorians.

Mr. Cook's shop consists of two rooms; his best books are in the second. There is a fine sense of age about the shop, and Cardinal Wolsey was born next door. From the second room a narrow staircase leads to a room which still clings to the fifteenth century. In those appropriate surroundings I found Father Clare, the secretary of the Irish Genealogical Society. With him was Mr. P. Paley whose knowledge of Irish genealogy was equally astounding. They were both of immense help to me. I put my case to them. I wanted the FitzGerald and Purcell family trees. In the middle of it I was interrupted by Mr. Cook, who had come up to tell me that a policeman wished to see me. I left Purcells, FitzGeralds, and much cigarette smoke and went downstairs. The policeman said I wasn't to leave the car outside the shop because the street was too narrow. He also objected to my having left the ignition key behind.

"They stole a car in Ipswich only yesterday," he said.

So I backed the car a few yards, which satisfied the policeman. Now the car was at the beginning of the street, which, after all, was not yet the street. I pocketed the ignition key, went upstairs, and by then the cigarette smoke had given up the ceiling as a bad job and settled down on books and old prints. I continued with my case.

Who were the FitzGeralds and where did they come from? That was soon answered.* The next ques-

* See Appendix A.

tion was who were the Purcells. That was more diffi-cult. Father Clare, Mr. Paley, and my wife began to examine different books. Naturally the Purcells were important for me. FitzGerald's father was John Pur-cell, who had married his cousin Mary Frances, daugh-ter of John FitzGerald and granddaughter of Keane FitzGerald of Totteridge, Herts., and John Purcell had changed his name to FitzGerald when his wife came into a large inheritance.

While the three of them busied themselves with the Purcell family tree, I took books down from the shelves at random, or lifted them off tables which were crowded with them, in the same haphazard fashion. Suddenly the name FitzGerald caught my eye. I began to read. It was from a pamphlet in the Brandshaw Collection, Cambridge University Library. I also saw the word Kildare. Was not FitzGerald a descendant of the Earls of Kildare? I sat down and copied out this confession of one Maurice FitzGerald who had been executed at Blessington on December 27, 1717. His could not have been a merry Christmas.

I Maurice FitzGerald was born in the county of Kildare and bred in the county of Carlow of very honest parents, and that my father Garrett FitzGerald was a gentleman in King James's army who by the misfortune of the world went to France after the surrender of Limerick and that for the want of friends or substance I missed the opportunity of learning or a trade, that for that reason I was obliged to go to serve the several persons following, viz. Wm. Brown, Wm Bumbery and John Humphries of the Co. of Carlow, gent, in whose several services I behaved myself very gentile and honest until the 9th May last that Hugh Connor a proclaimed rapparee impeached me for being in some robberies along with him, which when I understood to save my life I went to the road along with my fellow sufferers. I declare before God and the world that I never was guilty of any rogish rascally action nor of murder nor of robbing any poor traveller, man or woman, though I was betrayed by one John Reilly my own confederate and unfortunately taken by sergeant Alexander and his company of soldiers. I forgive the said Hugh Connor, John Reilly and all the world besides. I am about 27 years. I die a Roman Catholic. And the Lord have mercy upon my soul. Amen.

Maurice FitzGerald.

Certified true speech by Morgan Greed.

I was moved by Maurice FitzGerald's true speech, though it was quite possible that he had murdered. It was, in a sense, unimportant whether he was or was not a relation of Edward FitzGerald. Kinship, however vague, there must have been, at least in the days when the FitzGeralds, still with a small *g*, had come to Ireland; and curiously enough the first Fitzgerald, the grandson of Otho Geraldino, the one to cross to Ireland, was called Maurice too. But that was hardly in my thoughts. The last words of the "rapparee" evoked the picture of Ireland in the seventeenth and

15

eighteenth centuries, and from that Ireland Edward's family had come to England.

It was a hard, cruel, and oppressed land in which FitzGerald's ancestors were born, lived, suffered, and died. Perhaps no direct forebear of Edward Fitz-Gerald had "by the misfortune of the world" to go to France after the surrender of Limerick, but probably a neighbor did. It would be a pure matter of fancy to surmise that one of his family had been impeached for being in some robberies, but there were plenty on the road who were.

It is impossible to stand aside while history is being made—which, alas, is daily—but between Elizabeth and Cromwell an Irishman could do so a little. Cromwell stopped that and Dutch William made it impossible. Though FitzGerald was the child of Protestant parents he was the descendant of men and women who had been persecuted for their Catholic faith.

Thus my thoughts were running on when Mr. Cook appeared in the doorway. A policeman wished to see me.

I went downstairs. A somewhat taller policeman wished to see me this time. He told me I should not leave the car at the corner but park it in front of the bookshop. I drove the car a few yards forward, then wondered what to do with the ignition key. The policeman had already left, so I decided to leave it where it was, notwithstanding the stolen car of the day before.

Father Clare and Mr. Paley had in the meantime discovered a lot. They had found the Purcell family tree in the *Farnham Manuscripts,* Vol. VI, Part II, 1st Series.

"Never," said Father Clare, "has it been published before."

The actual family tree is in Appendix B, but because the details are more alive than names and dates, I made the following notes from the *Farnham Manuscripts,* notes which I do not think should be relegated to an appendix.

The Purcell family descends in a direct line from the old, distinguished race, the Purcells, Barons of Loughmoe, Co. Tipperary. Originally of Norman extraction, the first of the name who settled in England was a soldier of the Conquest and the first in Ireland, one of the companions of Henry II in his expedition to that country in 1172.

Within less than a century after, Sir James Ware in his Antiquities of Ireland relates that Sir Hugh Purcell, Knight, founded the convent of Francis Friars at Waterford, and was there buried. When James Butler, the 1st Earl of Ormonde and Ware, as Count Palatine of Tipperary, came to create Palatine Barons, he included among them the Purcells of Loughmoe and, thencefrom, the barons of Loughmoe ranked high on the role of local aristocracy. Intermarried with the Butlers of Ormonde and others of distinguished houses.

Nearer to us, John Purcell was born January 1, 1744, and married Eleanor, eldest daughter of John FitzGerald of Williamstown, and their eldest son was John Purcell, born December 25, 1775. This John Purcell, whose father was a rich Dublin doctor, had three sons, the second of whom was Edward Fitz-Gerald.

Edward's mother was a FitzGerald too. Thus his father and grandfather had each married a cousin. Whether his brother John's curious behavior, which at times bordered on madness, and his own eccentricity —which, however, produced one of the few clear flames which make this world worth while—had anything to do with this marrying of cousins seems highly probable.

But, as I wish to finish this complicated item of FitzGeralds and Purcells, this consideration can wait. John, Edward's father, changed his name by Royal License from Purcell to FitzGerald on September 23, 1823, and his son John, after John (formerly Purcell) FitzGerald's death, changed by Royal License his name to Purcell-FitzGerald—an almost full circle which makes one feel a little giddy.

Edward, himself, did not cherish the name Fitz-Gerald. It did not improve things for him when people began to mistake him for one Edward Marlborough FitzGerald. There is little known of Edward Marlborough FitzGerald save that he wrote some poetry, had been educated at Cambridge, got himself heavily in debt, lived with a washerwoman in the presence of five children, and that Thackeray offered him five pounds provided he left the country. While I was writing this book kind pople sent me poems written by Edward Marlborough FitzGerald, believing they were the work of Edward FitzGerald. One of Fitz-Gerald's biographers had been taken in by such poems. FitzGerald took to signing himself E. FG. in order not to be mistaken for Edward Marlborough. He did not much cherish his name either when Alfred Tennyson visited him at Woodbridge. On asking for FitzGerald's house, Tennyson was taken to the local police inspector whose name was also FitzGerald.

FitzGerald's father, a meek mild man, ended up in bankruptcy, trying to develop coal lands near Man-chester, which flooded. The man who bought the mines became rich, which is further proof of the father's inherent mildness. But FitzGerald's mother stands out, and from the distance of a hundred years and more still tries to overshadow husband and children, albeit with the father there was no need to try.

It is a curious fact that once one applies oneself to the study of the past and the dead, one comes up against the will power of the dead, long after they are expected to have disappeared with all their baggage. When I went into the old room at Boulge, I entered it *sine ire et studio,* for there was no reason for me to feel otherwise. Yet today I am a partisan and feel about most of the protagonists of this book as though I had spent a long week end with them in a house cut off from the road, thus having the opportunity to like or dislike them, as the case may be. Of Mary Frances I now know that she was a hard, formidable woman and it was no fun to be her husband or her child. Hers was an overbearing personality. She was considered a beauty; she was one of the richest commoners in the land; and her husband and children feared her and were in awe of her. She had inherited a considerable part of the fortune of her great-aunt, Mrs. Jane Joyce, who died in 1810 leaving property valued at between six and seven hundred thousand pounds.

Her grandfather, Kean FitzGerald, by his will directed the purchase of thousand-pound reduced 3 per cents, the dividends of which were to be distributed by the rector of East Barnet during the week before Christmas Day among thirty poor inhabitants of the parish of High Barnet who were not receiving parochial relief.

That is not much, but Edward's maternal grandfather had, in common with all the FitzGeralds, kindness of heart, which is charity itself. Edward's father had it; John, the brother, though often a laughing-stock, though quite intolerable, loved his neighbor dearly. Edward himself could tell a man who wished to repay a loan that he, for one, could not remember having lent him the sum, therefore no money should be returned to him.

It is unlikely that Mary Frances had much charity. She was an ostentatious woman, and Princess d'Ardia Caracceolo, brother John's great-granddaughter, who lives at the Island, County Waterford, which was one of Mary Frances's properties, told me that when Mary Frances was rowed from the mainland to the Island there were twenty-four musicians in the boat. A fine picture indeed, the elegance of the late eighteenth century blowing across the water from shore to house; but that splendid creature deserted her kind, aging husband when he was bankrupt and she still very rich.

Another tale came to me from Ireland: the Duke of Wellington had wanted to marry Mary Frances on account of her wealth. There is nothing to substantiate this tale, though the Duke might well have been the one man to curb that indomitable egotist.

Mary Frances had a box at the Haymarket, ate off gold plate, and the legend of the Duke of Wellington's wanting to marry her may be based on a drawing of her made by Lawrence. Of that drawing, FitzGerald wrote thus to Fanny Kemble in 1880:

My Sister Lusia's Widower has sent me a Drawing by Sir T. Lawrence of my Mother bearing a surprising resemblance to—the Duke of Wellington. This was done in her earlier days—I suppose not long after I was born—for her, and his [Lawrence's] friend Mrs. Wolff: and though, I think, too Wellingtonian, the only true likeness of her.

Fanny Kemble remembered her as a very handsome, clever, and eccentric woman whose fine house in Portland Place she greatly admired. When Fanny was young and Mr. FitzGerald's bankruptcy still in the offing, Mary Frances always wore a brooch with some of his hair in it, on the massive clasp of which were engraved the words: *Stessae sangre, stessa sorte*. When the coal-mine troubles began she forgot all about the blood, and fate for her consisted of leaving the man who was of the same blood.

Before she wearied of her husband she tired of the gold plate. It was replaced "by a set of round glass and dead and burnished silver, so exquisite that the splendid gold service was pronounced infinitely less tasteful and beautiful." Fanny Kemble truly admired her, which was not difficult since she was neither Mary Frances's husband nor child.

It is recorded that Mary Frances used to drive about in a carriage drawn by four black horses. In the Ipswich Public Library there is a letter from an old lady who had known her. In a trembling old handwriting she says she cannot remember the four black horses. Though I should have an open mind on that, though I know that in Suffolk four black horses stood in those days for the same idea that a fleet of Rolls-Royces stood even yesterday, I refuse to believe that Mary Frances could have driven about with less than four horses, and of course they were black. And one can well believe that one of the reasons the simple unostentatious life appealed to FitzGerald was not so much the four black horses and the gold plate as his mother's temperament.

Edward FitzGerald's life, topographically speaking, is a half-circle. That half-circle is round Woodbridge. It consists of Market Hill, Wherstead Lodge, Farlingay Hall, Bredfield House, Boulge Cottage, Boulge Hall, and Little Grange. Chronologically it is Bredfield House, Wherstead Lodge, Boulge Hall, Boulge Cottage, Farlingay Hall, Market Hill, and Little Grange, and there is no half-circle at all. Yet for me the name Boulge remains his center.

When I moved in at Boulge Hall, the daffodils had come out. They were yellow, of different hues and, in the sunshine, they were pure gold. From my study's window I saw a long carpet of daffodils, broken up here and there, stretching down to the stream, accompanied by trees on each side; on the other side of the stream in the distance was Boulge Wood. We used to have three stands there when we shot pheasants. And talking of pheasants—one day, out of an island of daffodils, there appeared an old cock pheasant. Fully aware that the shooting season had finished nearly four months before, he walked in slow royal procession with himself to the next island of daffodils. The sun, which was to go in about a fortnight in order to give way to a dismal summer, shone on his plumage, on the daffodils, and on the noisy ducks on the lake. I had by then peopled the lake with duck. There were Khaki Campbells, Aylesburys, and three remote strangers: a Muscovy drake and two Muscovy duck. The strangers—for strangers they remained to the last—kept aloof from the other duck. When the fleet of duck was out, swimming in formation, and met the Muscovies, it cut them dead.

The Muscovy drake was a coward and sat and trembled all the time. He seldom went into the water. One of his wives was a keen swimmer and struck up a friendship with a Khaki Campbell duck. The two girls would sit together for hours in some remote corner of the lake. That friendly Muscovy was the first to die; it wasted away. The drake became more of a coward. A little while after the great frost of '47 had started, the gardeners found the drake dead in the deep, frozen snow. They thought it was funny and revealing too that a Muscovite should die of cold in the English winter. The last of the Muscovites lost interest in the lake and would go every day further afield. In the beginning she was missed for an hour or so; then it was half a day.

One morning I was out early in the snow because the gamekeeper told me he had seen snipe the evening before, near one of the coverts Hasketon way, beside the frozen stream. We did not find or see the snipe but, as we came to the covert, the Muscovy was sitting on the frozen water. As I approached her a wild duck which had been keeping her company flew off. I was so surprised that I never fired at it. We waved and shouted to the Muscovy and she flew back to the lake. That afternoon she left again. Next day the gardener told me he saw her again with the wild duck. She was not far from the lake at the time, therefore the wild duck must have returned her call. Then she was never seen more.

The gardeners and I were convinced that after having lost her husband, having no kith or kin left on the lake, she decided to go off with the wild duck, for her wings had not been clipped as the wings of the other Muscovies, and so she was as free as any wild bird.

I often thought of her as flying off with the wild duck while the wind blew from the east, trying to churn up the solid icy snow. Perhaps the full moon, which FitzGerald often praised to Fanny Kemble, watched her, the white night, and her flight among free birds to some frozen marsh of liberty. But the gamekeeper said that in all probability the Muscovy had gone to another tame pond where the more astute new owner clipped her wings.

On second thought, FitzGerald's life was more like a horseshoe around Woodbridge which, wherever he lived, was always centered on Woodbridge. If you come out of the Bull Hotel on Market Hill you face the Shire House. On the right is a chemist, then a shop where I used to buy biscuits for my dogs. In that shop was a parrot; FitzGerald too had had a parrot. Next to the shop is a round blue tablet which says that FitzGerald had lived there. Since that house belongs to his middle age it is better for the moment not to take much notice of it. The street goes out to the By Pass at the corner of which is Farlingay Hall, but that too belongs to a later period. The By Pass takes one past a ruined lodge which is the lodge of Bredfield House where FitzGerald was born. The lodge had been demolished during the war of 1939–45 by a flying bomb. Nobody was hurt as the lodgekeeper and his wife were out at the time. Behind the trees that are behind the lodge stands Bredfield House. It is a Jacobean house of some architectural merit. It had been called Bredfield White House till a gentleman called White came to live there: Then it changed its name to Bredfield House. FitzGerald wrote a poem about it calling it Bredfield Hall.

When I lived in Suffolk, Bredfield House was empty. It is a curious thing that when, through my departure, Boulge became empty, all the homes Fitz-Gerald had had, with the exception of the Cottage, were vacant; for Bredfield House, Farlingay Hall, and Little Grange were empty too.

The FitzGeralds had come to Bredfield House, which they did not own but only rented, in order to wait for the day when they could move to Boulge which by then belonged to them. Why the FitzGer-ald family came to live in Suffolk is quite unknown. They already possessed plenty of property: a house in Portland Place, a manor house at Naseby called Naseby Woolleys, an estate and house at Seaford and one at Castle Irwell near Manchester, and also the Island in County Waterford. Yet they wanted one more in Suffolk which was, in those days as it is today, off the beaten track.

It is nowadays a petrifying thought to imagine oneself in possession of many establishments, packed with servants. Today one prefers to retreat into a shell, preferably with central heating; but in the early nineteenth century the world and the soul were not yet anemic. One wanted property, plenty of it, in order to enjoy it, glory in it, and then hand it down to one's children for their safekeeping. The glory was the well-appointed mansion, the long carriage drive, and masses of tenants. Property was a rising spiral which, when the century came to die, not only meant possession but the duty, too, to enlarge it, to add to it. It was the heir's duty to the departed parent to leave even more to his own heir.

Talking of my own experience in Suffolk, I should say that the first attack of the heirs came toward the seventies, the second by the heirs' heirs just before the First World War. John FitzGerald, Edward's brother, not long after taking over Boulge, began to enlarge the house. He added a new floor with dormer windows, thus killing the original simple Georgian structure of the house. The entrance, which was through the library, was not good enough for him: he built a new one with a porch and Gothic windows on the east side, and ever since then, when one comes up to the house, one's first impression is that one stands in front of a Victorian cloister.

In 1914 Boulge was enlarged again; the dining room was enlarged, the drawing room was enlarged, the morning room was added. In short, the house was made almost twice as large. It is a fine yet comic thought that, if the social structure of England had not changed, in two or three generations' time the Halls of Suffolk might have sprawled across the whole of Suffolk and as you left one you could immediately have entered another. Boulge, for example, would have met Bredfield House at the Pump Corner. Within another hundred years each house might have had a couple of thousand rooms, yet the ambitious heirs would have continued to build on. However silly and farfetched that sounds, there is something praiseworthy in such ambition.

So the reason why Mary Frances piloted her family into Suffolk was probably nothing else than the desire to possess more and more. One more estate was like having one more bracelet, or one more hair of her husband in the brooch. And the reason the family went to live at Bredfield House was to wait for Mrs. Short to die. Mrs. Short had no intention to do so. Boulge had belonged to Colonel and Mrs. Short. Who they were and where they came from nobody knows. They were not of Suffolk and consequently Suffolk had no interest in them. They are not buried at Boulge, neither at Bredfield nor at Debach. I tried hard to find out more about them but I came up against the wall which in Suffolk is speedily built round departed foreigners.

But what is known of them is not entirely uninteresting. The Colonel and his lady did not get on well with one another; in fact their lives were long cycles of silence spiced with hatred. At meals he would address only his dog, whereas the recipient of all her speech was the cat. The silent dining room with its candles and atmosphere of hatred is not an ineffective picture, especially if one adds the howling wind, the swaying trees, and the noise of the rooks in the rookery.

One proof of their mutual hatred has come down to us. It is the Cottage at the gate, which for sixteen years was FitzGerald's home. Mrs. Short had it built for the purpose of spending there, alone, those days or weeks when her husband's presence at the Hall was more unbearable than she had expected. In the end the Colonel died and she decided to sell the estate. The FitzGeralds bought it, but there was a clause in the agreement according to which Mrs. Short could remain at the Hall till her death. The FitzGeralds, first at Bredfield, then at Wherstead, and in Paris too, waited for her death. They had to wait for a long time.

Had it not been for the Shorts' unhappy marriage there would probably have been no Boulge Cottage, in which case FitzGerald would not have stayed long on the estate after his mother came into possession, for he would have looked for a quiet, simple home somewhere else. And speaking of estates and possessions which were so dear to his century, little Boulge Cottage is proof of the fact that in no way did FitzGerald share his fellows' love of property. When his brother John had become the squire of Boulge and had taken up residence at the Hall, he left the Cottage because it seemed to him his brother was too near; and he left it for Farlingay Hall, which was a farmhouse, and there he was but a lodger in the same manner as later in the rooms above the shop in Market Hill. He stood aside while the triumphant century with funnels, chimneys, smoke and mansions roared past him. But the wish to possess, if it does not come out in one thing, comes out in another. He did not want to own houses; he wanted to own his friends, and there are always the shallow and the cheap who do not mind being owned, of course for a consideration. But Fitz-Gerald is still a boy waiting with his family for Mrs. Short to die.

It was, as far as I know, the Colonel who built Boulge Hall around the year 1790. Some of the biographers refer to it as a Queen Ann house; Queen Ann was long dead when there was still no Boulge Hall.

One can easily picture the land of Boulge without the house. Undisturbed the sun shone on the oaks, the elms, beaches, chesnuts, and conifers. The large cedar which was to face my bedroom window, provided it was already there, must have lorded it in freedom. That cedar will always live in my memory, for during the icy winter of '47 every morning when I opened my eyes its branches seemed more and more to be laden with snow. In that winter you would not have been surprised, had the lake not been frozen, to see seals swimming in it. But the cedar was the true symbol of the frost. I almost expected it to break through the walls and, with its ever-increasing load of snow, come, like the statue in a play on Don Juan I saw many years before in Seville, clattering into the house to bring the winter even nearer. In winter, before there was Boulge Hall, the landscape must have been forlorn yet majestic, and when the sun shone on the silent snow it was surely beautiful and the paired-off partridges "chizzicked" in the sun.

In order to find out about the origin of Boulge I again consulted Father Clare. The name itself is curious. It is not a pretty word; in fact it could sound positively rude. For instance, if one said, "I boulged him properly," one would not imagine something dignified or elegant. One version is that the word Boulge originates from the Norman word *bouge* which means heather, thus implying there must have been heather at Boulge. As the land is heavy clay there never was any heather. So that explanation does not fit. I would agree with Mr. Arnott of Woodbridge, who has studied and written about the origins of place-names in the Deben valley, that in all probability there had been a tribe of Saxons called the Boulges long before Suffolk became Holy Suffolk.

Father Clare put me on to Copinger's *Manors of Suffolk*. In Volume VIII I found the history of the Manor of Boulge, and there is the list of the men who went before the FitzGeralds came:

Odo de Campania	Doomsday survey
? Robert Mallet	
Bovilles	Henry III
Queen Margaret	1281
Sir John Boville	
William Boville	same reign
Sir John de Seckford	1334
Sir George Seckford	
It remained in the Seckford family until 1673 when Dorothy, widow of Henry Seckford, left the manor to Sir Henry North, her cousin.	
Henry William Bunbury	1776
Thomas Emerson the younger & William Whiscop	1779
William Whitby	1790
Henry & Eleanor Short	1798

Thus we are back to the Shorts. Coppinger goes on to say:

The manor was shortly afterwards purchased by John FitzGerald son of John FitzGerald of Williamstown, Co. Waterford. He married Mary, only daughter of Keane Fitz-Gerald of Totteridge, Herts., and had a son Charles who married Louisa Denvers and died without issue September 1807, and a daughter Mary Frances. John FitzGerald, High Sheriff for Counties Kent and Waterford, besides the family estates, succeeded to estates in Lancashire and Staffordshire under the will of his relation Richard FitzGerald who married a daughter and a co-heir with her sister Catherine, Countess of Fauconberg, of William Fowler of St. Thomas, County Stafford. John FitzGerald died on 6th September 1818 when the manor passed to his only daughter Mary Frances FitzGerald. She inherited a considerable portion of the fortune of her great-aunt Mrs. Jane Joyce who died in 1810 leaving property to the amount of between £600,000 and £700,000. She married her first cousin John Purcell M.D. of Kilkenny, eldest son of John Purcell of Dublin by Eleanor, eldest daughter of John FitzGerald of Williamstown.

It is almost annoying how one returns to Mary Frances even when one tries to find out who had owned Boulge Manor long before her day. With her Wellingtonian aspect, the Iron Duchess herself, she is astride the life of Boulge and her son Edward. Till her death she was, one feels certain, the frightening and dominating influence in his life. He did his best to be away from her as often as possible. To be sitting with her in her box at the theater must have been an awe-inspiring experience. It was preferable to be in the distance. But to run from a person one fears is now and then a closer bond than remaining put in the overwhelming presence.

One's own life often gives opportunities to understand better the dead or living neighbor; and therefore, when I think of the relationship between Mary Frances and her second son, I invariably remember a fear and hatred of my early life. In my case it was a man. Fear and dislike of him was like a cloud; then at last I burst through that cloud and ran. I ran as far as the Argentine, and one day I was sitting in the dining car of the French Railway, the train going from Santa Fé to Rosario. I sat down, looked up, and there facing me was a man who very much resembled the person I feared. The resemblance began to weigh on me, then it grew and enveloped me. I could not go on sitting there, so I took myself and the plate of soup and went to sit at another table with my back to him. That did not help either. I felt his presence behind me and I had to turn round and look at him. That complete stranger had by then become conscious of my panic. Our eyes met and his were triumphant. I could not finish my meal. I paid and returned to my compartment. It would be a fitting ending to the story if the man had suddenly appeared in the compartment, sat down, and watched me cringing in my seat. However,

I did not see him again and only my fear, which was enough, remained with me till the end of the journey.

So FitzGerald's roaming and absences during his mother's life could not have been lighthearted. Once when she drove her four black horses in mid-term to Trinity College, Cambridge, in order to see him for one reason or other, he sent the excuse that, as he had only one pair of shoes which at the moment were at the cobbler, he could not appear barefooted in her presence.

His biographers refer to that incident as something delightful which proves how frugal a young fellow he was: the emphasis is of course on the one pair of shoes. It did not occur to them that FitzGerald might have been so petrified by the news of his mother's arrival that the excuse of one pair of shoes and those at the cobbler was thought out by a frightened mind which, out of sheer fear, could invent no better excuse.

The childhood at Bredfield could not have been an unhappy one. There were holidays to Aldeborough, where the bathing machine is apparently still the same one. Huge and heavy, no later age could have produced it. At Bredfield there were Mary Frances, five sisters, two brothers, the mild father, and his mild friend, Mr. Jenny of Haskerton, who eventually was ruined and died as a result of the bankruptcy of Fitz-

Gerald's father. Mr. Jenny came home one day, called out he was ruined, went to bed and died. FitzGerald was devoted to him. The children were now and then beaten, and they played and romped about as most children do.

Let it not be thought that Mary Frances was a sort of monster. She had a liking for her own jokes, one of which survived. In a letter to Aldis Wright, his literary testator-to-be, in 1876 FitzGerald said, ". . . which could offend the chastest Eye or Ear, as my mother used to quote from the Advertisement to a Puppet Show."

"Which," one imagines Mary Frances saying, "could offend the chastest eye or ear."

She would look round with eagle eyes, and the five daughters and three sons, pulled by those eyes like puppets, would heehaw to the mother's satisfaction. In the background the obscure father would pretend he was giggling.

Undoubtedly it was not an unhappy childhood, nor do I wish to insinuate that it was. Children are seldom completely miserable. To FitzGerald nothing was a reality before it belonged to the past; then he could color it and sigh over it. Bredfield to him remained a pleasant memory, which is the most one can ask from one's childhood.

His father and Squire Jenny shared the costs of a

pack of harriers; that for the children was surely fun. Mary Frances was often away, which was even more fun. There were shrubs in front of the house, and behind these little Edward hid, when his mother came or went, to have an undisturbed quiet view of her, of the coach of a good full yellow color, and of the four black horses.

Another friend of his father was Major Moor of Great Bealings. Major Moor, from a small boy's point of view, had many accomplishments. The Major, as a cadet of thirteen, had seen the *Royal George* go down. His walking stick was made of wood of the *Royal George*. It must have been an exceptional walking stick. The Major collected Indian gods. He had a fine array of them at Bealings and the boy often saw them and admired them. It has been suggested with disarming ease that the sight of those idols contributed to FitzGerald's desire in later life to translate the Rubáiyát. When I first read of that I made this note: "Major Moor and his Eastern Idols may have influenced his [FitzGerald's] wish to translate the Rubáiyát. Rubbish—Cowell was the man. Youthful idols—like steam engines and puffer trains—do they make a Stevenson?"

I could have added that FitzGerald's interest in the East was not as tangible as Major Moor's idols. Nevertheless, it is difficult to know what remains behind from childhood impressions. The child genius might become a station master and the clergyman's pious son a murderer. It is unlikely that when FitzGerald sat down and wrote:

Awake! For Morning in the Bowl of Night
Has flung the Stone that puts the Stars to Flight—

the idols of the Major walked out of his unconscious and ran through the pages. Unlikely indeed, and that is all that can be said.

I was hardly installed at Boulge when I was told one morning that two ladies were wandering round the grounds and one of them was, so she had said, a grand-niece of FitzGerald. I sent the ladies the message that it would please me if they came in, but the grand-niece said she would not come in. So I went out.

From the very start she eyed me with suspicion, and urbanity was lacking in her manners. I asked if she would have a drink as it was past noon. She said no. Conversation, I saw, would have to be all of my making, and while I spoke she walked about inspecting this, scrutinizing that, and taking as little notice of me as the circumstances allowed. Because I did not know what to say, I said, "I am seriously thinking of writing a life of FitzGerald."

"You mustn't do that," she said.

"Why?" I asked, not unduly surprised.

"Because I wouldn't give you permission to write a book about him. I know the sort of book you would write."

"What sort of book?"

"Like Lytton Strachey."

I was flattered, but she went on to say that she had already given permission to Mr. Terhune to write a life of FitzGerald and she knew that she would be satisfied with his book. There the lady was not wrong, for with all due respect, Mr. Terhune's *Life* is truly a book for grandnieces. I murmured something about no permission being needed, which did not go down well either. Then I made the mistake of the day.

"I am terribly fascinated by him," I said. "I feel there is some mystery attached to him."

"I knew it," she cried. "Of course a person like you would say there is a mystery attached to him. There is no mystery. He was an Irish gentleman with a thousand a year. There is no mystery whatever. All those stories of his being an eccentric aren't true either. Not a bit true."

I murmured she was perfectly right. An Irish gentleman with a thousand a year would have no mysteries; nor would he, of course, be an eccentric. Then she told me she wanted to go to the church and the grave. I offered to accompany her. She did not thank me but marched past the chickens, the orchard, the rookery, and then into the church. The noise of the rooks was deafening. She stayed on in the church. As it was well past luncheon time and she did not need my services, I went back to the house. In the afternoon I furtively looked into the church, but she had gone.

I was angry and, since anger is no wise counselor, I decided that I would act on my impulse and write a book about FitzGerald. To be a genius is a mystery itself, and to have such curious flashes of genius as FitzGerald had was very much a mystery.

I woke up that night; a little later Old Nelly, the stable clock, chimed four. There is a mystery attached to Old Nelly too, for if my informants were right about the date the Hall was built, then, like the prophet's coffin, Old Nelly must have floated above the not-yet-built stables for about fifteen years, because the clock was made and presumably installed in 1768.

Why her name is Old Nelly perhaps FitzGerald would know, though were he nowadays in the position to explain anything, there are other questions I should put to him, most of which he might leave unanswered. Old Nelly's chimes are sad chimes. FitzGerald called them lugubrious.

So the stable clock chimed four. Now and then Fitz-Gerald must have awakened at that hour and counted the strokes too. From an old plan of the house I knew that my bedroom had been Mary Frances's drawing room and my dressing room her bedroom. The nursery wing had not then existed, therefore the children, who were by then well grown up, were in all likelihood packed into the east wing. There was not much need for imagination to picture FitzGerald as he awoke. He was beginning to get bald and his countenance had either "a smiling air" or a "pathetic droop of the brows which gave the face a sadder expression, more like his later look." If only, I thought, with the memory of the niece still with me, I knew what was in his mind while he listened to the chimes I could start on that book with more confidence; and my mind tried to pierce a mind that had thought in that house a hundred years before. It was like trying to find an opening in a wall which had crumbled long before.

Later Old Nelly chimed five. The clock infuriated me. The same chimes, the same hours, yet the fact that we both had listened to them brought us not together. What annoyed me chiefly was that I could visualize the other members of the family with comparative ease. John, who by the time they had come to Boulge was under the influence of Matthews, the Bedfordshire evangelist who blew a trumpet to let his flock know that one of his sermons of hyacinth and brimstone was about to begin, was easily recognizable in the gloom of the dawn. Peter, too; but not the man I had continuously in my thoughts.

I tried again. When they came to Boulge, FitzGerald, though still young, had already acquired the love of yesterday. Nothing was good enough till it was of the past. The ideal thing in life is to enjoy the present, have pleasant memories of the past, and await hopefully, albeit not impatiently, the future. For him the future, whether his or England's, was generally bleak. Tomorrow had no meaning till it changed into yesterday. He was twenty years old when he wrote:

> *Then with an old friend*
> *I talk of our youth—*
> *How 'twas gladsome but often*
> *Foolish forsooth:*
> *But gladsome, gladsome!*

Even if the fastidious ear might object to the word "gladsome," those are the words of one who looks back on youth from the disillusioned distance of middle age at least. Yet they were written by a very young man, which should be the apology for "gladsome" but does not explain the sadness. As I go along I will quote the entire poem, "The Meadows of Spring," for it not only gave me the title of this study but it is an elegant thing and will always remain for me the picture of the cycle of the seasons as I saw it at Boulge.

So there, I continued, he had been lying in bed on

43

the same floor, listening to Old Nelly, thinking of the past. He could get infinite pleasure out of the past. The past for the moment was probably Bredfield House, his childhood home. Bredfield House is just over a mile from Boulge Hall and, if you do not take the road which twists round Pump Corner but cross the fields, it is somewhat less. Instead of waiting for the morning and walking over to see it as it was, he let his imagination build it up out of the clouds of the past. This is not speculation on my part: a letter of his rather throws light on my point. In October 1839 he wrote to Bernard Barton, the Quaker poet of Woodbridge:

Thank you for the picture of my dear old Bredfield which you have secured for me: it is most welcome. Poor Nursey once made me a very pretty oil sketch of it: but I gave it to Mr. Jenny. By all means have it engraved for the pocket book: it is well worthy. Some of the tall ash trees about it used to be visible at sea: but I think their topmost branches decayed now. This circumstance I put in, because it will tell in your verse illustration of the view. From the road before the lawn, people used plainly to see the topmasts of the men-of-war lying in Hollesley bay during the war, I like the idea of this: the old English house holding up its enquiring chimneys and weathercocks (there is great physiognomy in weathercocks) towards the far-off sea and the ships upon it. . . .

I went and stood on the road before the lawn; I ascertained the measurements of the highest masts during

44

the Napoleonic wars. I asked the oldest inhabitants whether the landscape could have changed as much as that, and the definite conclusion I was compelled to draw was that nobody could have seen the masts of the ships-of-the-line from that road before the lawn. He did not see them himself while he had lived at Bredfield House, but the masts rose once Bredfield was of the past; and so later rose the sultan's turret. The sorrow and guilt of today sat heavily on him; yesterday was a thing of beauty because one could no longer interfere with it. The turmoil of today was distasteful; moreover, it demanded a certain amount of exertion, and Fitz-Gerald was not good at that.

Before leaving Bredfield House, let that same letter wave good-by to it. "How well I remember," FitzGerald wrote, "when we used all to be in the Nursery and from the window see the hounds come across the lawn, my Father and Mr. Jenny in their hunting-caps etc. with their long whips—all Daguerreotyped into the mind's eye now—and that is all . . ."

Then suddenly, as I lay in bed thinking of minarets and masts, Old Nelly chimed nine o'clock. It was of course only half-past five. But the old clock was often capricious. A friend of mine, an eminent critic and writer of merit, spending a week end with me, told me reproachfully one Sunday morning that Nelly had struck ten around three in the morning. I apologized

45

and explained that she could not be blamed entirely for she had fallen on hard times. In the past, during the days of the Shorts, the FitzGeralds, and the Whites, hers was a well-regulated existence. She knew that if she struck twelve at midnight, say on November the 18th, in twenty years' time at the same moment it would be midnight again. Nowadays, what with Summer Time and Double Summer Time, the poor old clock had become bewildered. I am not quite certain whether my friend saw my point.

I went on the stroke of nine to the window but it was still dark outside. Beneath me were two gravel paths, each on a different terrace. The top terrace was, as it were, held by a brick wall camouflaged by lavender. Later we had the lavender cut out, also some decaying rose bushes before it; when the roses had gone, tobacco plants, the existence of which we had not suspected, grew wild and glorious in the morning and the evening but became sleepy in the day. During the hot dry summer of '47 their scent and their white color were a fine atonement for the yellow grass stretching thirstily to the woods.

On the top path, outside the dining room, the ghosts of Boulge are supposed to promenade. Needless to say, the ghosts are none other than the Colonel and his lady. Thomas Wright, who wrote a copious, ill-informed life of FitzGerald, had the saving grace to admit that, though he had spent a whole night's vigil, he did not see the Shorts. In the beginning I had flattered myself that my eyes might be more receptive than Thomas Wright's. Alas, I saw them neither. There are moments when one would gladly see a ghost; I, too, had such moments, but the Shorts remained invisible.

Local gossip since Wright's time had gone one better on the Shorts. Apparently, if you walk on the road to the home farm, or cut across the field behind the Fitz-Gerald family vault, and provided it is late at night, you will see a tall, broad, bald-headed figure with a sad though severe aspect, walking along lanes and across the fields. That is FitzGerald. Truly he had cut across the field between church and home farm and thus must often have passed the spot where ultimately he was buried, for he visited frequently with Mr. Smith of the home farm, whose son Alfred was to become both his reader and friend, but neither in later life nor after death did he walk there again. The head gardener at Boulge often crossed that field at night, so did the gamekeeper and the cowman; and I am certain they would have told me of him had they seen him. Alas, once more, he does not haunt Boulge.

Yet there is something haunting and inexplicable about Boulge, not only in the trees and the wild flowers, but also in that curious fact that even a hundred years ago the population of Boulge was under fifty. Now it is about thirty, and since our departure less than that. It has a church and, though now it is half empty, on a Sunday before the Black Death it must have been full. Some day when big houses, including Boulge, have all been pulled down, there will be perhaps a few farm laborers left, and then when the Minister of Health of the day decides to build a satellite town for Woodbridge, the oaks will have to go too.

During the winter of '47 on a morning when the sky was of a darker color than the white fields, the butler came to tell me that he had some terrible news. The daily woman from Debach, who on account of the frozen snow had come not on bicycle but on foot, saw as she crossed the churchyard that the door of the Fitz-Gerald crypt was open.

"That," he said, "means that somebody has burgled the grave."

His eyes rolled; he was given to fear. What happened was, as I discovered later, that the cold had burst the dilapidated door open. The cold would let not even the dead rest in peace. But that day I saw a heron flying toward Cyprus Covert: it was a consoling sight.

During our last few months at Boulge, when we were without a living-in staff, there were only my wife and I who slept in the house. Therefore, had I heard any noise in the night, it would have meant either burglars or ghosts. However, no burglars and no ghosts came, and if there was a stealthy sound in the night it was Celia the cat bringing an offering of mouse, rat, or baby rabbit for her kittens which had been taken away from her; but she, long after their departure, was still convinced that if she hoarded food for them they would return in time. Corridors and rooms were daily littered with the offerings which, in a sense, came not from the fields but from a broken mother's heart.

However much one wishes to probe the mystery of a man who, according to his grandniece, had no mystery attached to him, one has to concentrate first on the first mystery, which is birth. That mystery is followed by childhood, which in FitzGerald's case entailed a stay in Paris. In 1816, when he was seven years old, he was taken by his father to France, where they lived at Saint Germain-en-Laye, then in Paris.

The age of seven is already very much one of the formative years. Impressions bore themselves deep in, and from that depth rise the flames of imagination. Now FitzGerald at that age was in a Catholic country, and fundamentally France was as Catholic then as it is today. In a Protestant country one has the boredom of the Sabbath at one's elbow and the Salvation Army band beside one's ear, but in Catholic lands one cannot go far enough not to hear the bells calling to Mass.

There are, moreover, certain Catholic attributes one cannot escape, especially in one's formative years. Though he was to spend his life mostly in "doubting castle" and was to produce for the rationalists their anthem, namely the Rubáiyát, certain Catholic principles entered Fitz-Gerald's soul during his stay in France, the most important of them being the Church's conception of charity, which he practiced whenever he could.

I know one can be dishonest and consequently convincing if one takes a line here, a passage there, to prove one's point. For example, with a man who has written as many letters as FitzGerald, by taking certain sentences out of their context I could turn him into a Fascist or Communist were I so disposed; therefore, when I speak of his Catholic conception of charity, I do not wish to give the impression that he was a Catholic, practicing or otherwise, because that would be untruthful. Nevertheless, he was nearer to it than he himself supposed. When his brother turned Catholic, he showed true understanding. Still, it was in charity that he approached Catholicism.

". . . what think you," he wrote in a letter to Fanny Kemble in 1873, "of these lines of Clément Marot on the Death of some French Princess who desires to be buried among the Poor?"

Probably Fanny Kemble thought nothing of them, and few people would, apart from those who understand the Church's conception of charity. The lines are by Marot, Cimetière XXVII:

> *De Damoyselle Anne de Marle*
>
> . . . .
>
> *Lors sans viser au lieu dont elle vint,*
> *Et desprisant la gloire que l'on a*
> *En ce bas monde icelle Anne ordonna,*
> *Que son corps fust entre les povres mys*
> *En ceste fosse. Or prions, chers amys,*
> *Que l'ame soit entre les povres mise*
> *Qui bien-heureux sont chantez en l'église.*

I grant this is little evidence, but FitzGerald did practice charity. Those lines of Marot would surely have left good Protestant brother John unmoved. They can appeal only to one whose ears are not completely deaf to the church bells which FitzGerald heard day in, day out, in France.

While in Saint-Germain he saw Louis XVIII out hunting in the forest, he saw Monsieur who was to become Charles X, the royal guard in green and gold; but what remained paramount in his memory about his trips to France was a man he saw on the Boulevard by the Madeleine, in 1830 in Paris a little before the revolution, a man:

. . . who was singing to his Barrel-organ. Several passing "Blouses" had stopped also: not only to listen, but to join in the Songs, having bought little "Libretti" of the words from the Musician. I bought one too; for, I suppose, the smallest French Coin, and assisted in the Song which the Man called out beforehand (as they do Hymns in Church), and of which I enclose you the poor little Copy. "Le Bon Pasteur, s'il vous plait." I suppose the Circumstances: the "beau temps", the pleasant Boulevards, the then so amiable People, all contributed to the effect this Song had upon me; anyhow it has constantly revisited my memory for these forty-three years; and I was thinking, the other day, touched me more than any of Beranger's most beautiful Things.

This, however, may be only one of "Old Fitz's Crotchets" as Tennyson and others would call them.

It would be a crotchet, too, if I emphasized that the refrain of the song was: *"Et le bon Dieu vous benira."* It is noteworthy that in the delightful picture of the Boulevard his reference to the people of Paris, whom, when he wrote the letter, he had not seen for a donkey's year nor would see ever again, was "the then so amiable People." They could not be amiable today but, like everything else for him, they had been splendid the day before yesterday.

I cannot help asking myself whether that love of yesterday was not simply a form of defense for one who lived mostly in the country, where most pleasures are similar to the chewing of the cud, that is to say, where most pleasures are identically the same and repeat themselves with the regularity of the sun and the moon. This is not meant to detract from those pleasures, but the fact is that days are seldom separated from the week, and if you say you enjoyed the spring or the autumn you refer in your thoughts to a cycle of days lit up by the same sun, which is all you remember of the season. July has not thirty-one individual days: it is just July.

Market day or a trip to town stands out; and then one waits, pleasantly of course, for next market day or next trip to town. The countryman himself is kept busy with the land, his beasts and crops; the sportsman has his fishing, shooting, and hunting; FitzGerald cultivated no land and he was not keen on field sports. He loved flowers but was no gardener; he sailed on his boat but did not sail it.

The days at Boulge, in the depth of the country, or at Woodbridge, where he stood aloof from the local pursuits of selling corn and coal, working in shops and offices, were often too long. One cannot write, read, and study all the time. Loneliness can be irritating and Fitz-Gerald had a true gift for being irritated. Of his beloved, boring small town of Woodbridge he exclaimed in utter disgust in one of his many undated letters to Aldis Wright, ". . . I shall be at Woodbridge but you know I don't advise anyone to go *there* unless on the road elsewhere."

At Boulge and at Woodbridge he assembled any company that would give him its time. There was plenty of small fry among it, but not even solicitor and bank clerk could be continuously at his beck and call. However fascinating and lucrative it was for Bernard Barton, the Quaker-poet bank clerk, and for Thomas Churchyard, the solicitor and bad painter, to hover round him, their pursuits in banks and offices, in the hard beds with huge eiderdowns, and at the fumed-oak family tables would leave him frequently alone.

When thus alone he could cherish the past and, cherishing it, he turned it into his armor against loneliness and boredom. Memory is peopled with inaccessible faces beckoning from the distance. He was alone; the past shone. If at Boulge there was only the hooting of the owls, if at Woodbridge only the last belch of the last drunk leaving the tap of the Bull, he sat down and wrote his letters, which are among the finest in the language. Boredom, that civilized grace, is responsible for many masterpieces; in FitzGerald's case it deserves our gratitude on account of the letters.

But let it not be thought that he was no true lover of the countryside which, for him, was inevitably Suffolk. He could not have been happy for long anywhere else. It seems possible that during his short and acutely unhappy marriage he was chiefly in London, for the understandable reason that going the whole hog of misery was the sole remedy. He loved the fields, trees, and flowers. He had an admiring understanding of the countryman's delightful coarseness, his idiom and his resourcefulness. In his old age he was still amused when he heard that a farmer had invited a friend "to dine off an Arse of Beef & Hamper of Greens." He reported that at once to his friend Aldis Wright, later the stern Vice-Master of Trinity.

His criticism was often harsh and therefore quite unjust. He believed in debunking and hated people and thoughts he considered sham. The wind of East Anglia rips off the velvet, and many a dainty slipper has found itself in one or the other of the deep ditches in which Suffolk specializes.

One such experience of debunking comes to mind, an experience FitzGerald would have enjoyed. There was in my time a man in Woodbridge, pleasant and given to exaggeration. Among other things he told me he had bought a greyhound which he assured me was the best greyhound in the world. After a while his persistent boasts became tedious, so I jumped at his suggestion that he bring the animal to Boulge and show me what the best greyhound could do. He arrived with the greyhound and there was a certain amount of preliminary conversation which went something like this:

"Don't forget, sir," the owner said, "that if she catches a hare or a rabbit she'll tear it to pieces. Otherwise I'd of course give it to you."

"Very kind of you," I said politely.

"I wouldn't," he said, "like to be in any old 'are's shoes with her after 'im."

I said I appreciated that, and then we set out. We went toward Boulge Wood. In the field, which was the cemetery of oats trodden to the ground by the rain and hail of the disastrous summer, there usually was some game. The greyhound walked gingerly, looked this way, stared that way, and a hare got up and made for the wood.

"Look, a hare!" he shouted to the greyhound. The greyhound did not look. He explained to me she was still unaccustomed to the idea but would soon pick it up. She did pick it up when a rabbit bolted from the oats, for she went after it, though unhurried.

"Never mind," he said. "She begins to know what it's all about."

We opened the gate and entered the wood. There was a long ride before us. A pigeon detached itself from a tree with a sudden rustle of leaves, a noisy pest of a jay flew off, and then the greyhound rushed after a rabbit. The owner was in ecstasy. There was no getting away from it: the greyhound was slowly gaining on the rabbit. Then an amazing thing happened. Like one of

56

those colorful balls in a circus, which with a sudden bang emits a Union Jack and a Star-Spangled Banner, the rabbit became two rabbits. One ran down a hole on the left; the other, which had been sitting unperceived beside the wire fence that is supposed to protect the plantation of saplings, climbed across the wire netting. The approaching greyhound looked right, then left, and eventually stopped.

"That wasn't her fault," the owner said. "She was flummoxed, the poor girl."

I admitted it was no fault of hers, though, if she had been a little faster, she could have got the first rabbit before it reached the second. The owner now again spoke in praise of her. She had acted wonderfully, she had spotted the rabbit which had been in the shadow, her speed had been wonderful. It was stupid, of course, that there had been two rabbits—unexpected, too. The torrent of his words was fast washing away the greyhound's poor performance. A magpie, aware that I had no gun, flew over, and a cock pheasant was talking deeper in the wood.

"Look," I said, for it was at last my turn.

The greyhound had lain down. She lay, poor thing, her tongue hanging, her brindle body shaking with breaths that were like sobs. He could not make her rise. He talked to her, implored her, but could not make her rise. He prodded her and while he prodded her explained

57

that, after a short rest, she would catch the first rabbit or hare. Nothing made the greyhound rise, and in the end he had to carry her back to his car. On their way back he disturbed a hare, which he pretended not to notice, and the greyhound did not care.

The story of the man with the greyhound is no far cry from FitzGerald. He lived among men like that; he understood them, loved them, and was amused by them. The ground of the greyhound's defeat had been his ground, too.

With a sudden shock I notice that FitzGerald is still a small boy and I have not yet sent him to school. But, before sending him off with his brothers to Doctor Malkin's school at Bury St. Edmunds, there are a few more things to be said of his childhood. The first of them was said by his sister, Mrs. Wilkinson, some time after Fitz-Gerald's death.

I remember [she said] when my Mother read to us anything interesting, he [Edward] used to creep under the table to feed on and enjoy what she read. . . . He shared in common with us the lessons of a worthy French master, a Dancing Master who would sometimes escape from teaching us a Minuet to join some procession to the Church and was a beautiful dancer, grace and ease characterised all his movements. He with my two brothers had a Fencing Master, one of Napoleon's old Guard who wanted to make warriors of them all but to no effect . . .

That, of course, was still in Paris. It is a pity that Mrs. Wilkinson speaks only of the grace and ease of the Dancing Master, for it would be a nice thing to know how FitzGerald danced the Minuet.

Mrs. Wilkinson's husband was a clergyman. Alfred Tennyson liked to believe that he himself was the author of that Wordsworthian line: "A Mr. Wilkinson, a clergyman," but FitzGerald pointed out that the honor of that line went to him and not to the Laureate, because when he had heard that his sister Jane was to marry a Mr. Wilkinson who was a clergyman, he wrote that line in the best vein of Daddy Wordsworth. The Wilkinsons lived for a while in Florence and made serious efforts to convert the Papists to the Church of England. FitzGerald's comment was: "I suppose, as the Yorkshireman said, it amuses her and doesn't hurt them."

Little Edward could sit for long over a solitary flower in a glass of water and watch it unfold, not because he was botanically minded but simply because the beauty of it appealed to him. Already, as a young boy, he was imbued with charity, and at Wherstead there was a poor old woman with a "nutcracker" face, whom he used regularly to visit, sit with, talk to, and thus much delight her.

Once on a winter day the children were going to start for a drive in the open phaeton. The wind blew the cold and the snow across the Orwell. Little Edward thought as they got in that the footman who sat behind them would naturally be cold. That is not difficult to notice on such a day, but few people have eyes for such details, especially when they themselves are well wrapped up. Edward told the footman to fetch the purple surtout which hung in the hall. When it arrived, he turned round to his sister Jane and said, "Charles and I divide this coat between us."

Shrouded in the purple surtout, Charles the footman, it is good to record, shared during that drive and supposedly many other drives, in more ways than one, Fitz-Gerald's immortality.

FitzGerald's father said the boy had plenty of fun in him, and he was always ready to make droll speeches. A Miss Mary Lynn, who had known him in the course of the Aldeborough holidays, remembered him as a little boy who liked quiet fun, was not fond of field sports, but played whist and piquet. Napoleon's old guard must have disapproved of that. But now to school.

Part Two

THE THREE brothers, John, Edward, and Peter, were sent to the King Edward VI Grammar School at Bury St. Edmunds, the headmaster of which was Doctor Malkin. The boys liked him and were devoted to Mrs. Malkin. John was not a gay boy. Gaiety could hardly have been expected from the future author of such pamphlets as *Plain Advice on Drinking and Drunkenness, Account of the Death of Lord Hill Killed While Hunting at Bramford Park March 1844,* and *Lines Addressed to J. Kirkman Esq. M.D. upon His Retirement from the Governorship of Melton Asylum.*

Peter was different, for he was gay though no scholar. His joy at Bury was to meet the London coach because he was allowed to handle the ribbons. He was a dashing driver; his driving frightened the passengers, complaints were lodged with Doctor Malkin, who forbade Peter any more handling of ribbons, but like the kindly simple soul he was, Peter did not let himself be outdone. He was soon seen driving a hearse with four plumed horses and, when the sensible headmaster was informed, his dry comment was: "I don't see any need to interfere unless the passenger complains."

It is possible that Peter FitzGerald's love of driving coaches was in his blood. An uncle in Ireland, Peter Purcell, whom Edward much liked, had made a fortune out of running all the stagecoaches in Ireland in partnership with a Scotsman who, when he died, left him his money. Perhaps the example of his uncle fired Peter's imagination when he drove the hearse.

Edward FitzGerald was happy at school. To use the time-worn cliché, he received a good grounding in the Classics, and his pleasure in the Classics remained with him for the rest of his long life. Doctor Malkin was also a lover of English literature. He was keen on essays and, as Fanny Kemble records (her brother was at the school at the same time), the essays which gained approbation were honored with a place in a series of large volumes entitled *Musae Burienses*.

The year FitzGerald entered the school one subject was: "Mr. Hogarth's compliments to Mr. King and requests the honour of his company to dinner on Thursday next to Eta Beta Pi." Another was: "At her feet he bowed." John FitzGerald gained honors in the second by comparing the poetry of the Hebrews with that of Pindar and other Greek lyrists.

Mr. Terhune in his *Life of FitzGerald* gives an analysis of his career at Bury. In the first form he was first of twenty-one students, in the second thirteenth of twenty-one students, then third and tenth and twelfth and fourth. For me, however, more telling are FitzGerald's words to Adelaide Kemble when talking of Mrs. Malkin: "Oh, you can never know how charming she was; you were never a schoolboy in her care."

One thing is certain, whether fourth or tenth, he was not a problem child. The hermit-to-be, the man at whose passing fools would tap their foreheads, was not a misunderstood weak boy. It must be stressed that he was all his life a man of robust health, though it is true that in old age he had bronchial trouble and his eyes, now and then, yet not as often as he thought, weakened from too much reading. It is important when one tries to understand a person to dwell on his health and general physical condition. Bad health has an overriding influence in either this or that direction. With FitzGerald the question of bad health is nonexistent. He never suffered from a major disease and he was throughout life an active man. When he read, he often walked up and down; he was by no means a languid man feasting only off his intellect.

It is amusing to record that some time before I started

this book I asked a woman friend who, like so many others, knew precisely nothing of FitzGerald, how she thought the man of Omar Khayyám fame had looked.

"Thin, very handsome, with a lot of fair hair," she replied.

She also, I suppose, imagined him reclining on a sofa.

She was disappointed when I told her that FitzGerald was burly, bear-like, bald, and incredibly tough, for when he fell from his boat into the sea and was pulled out, he refused to change or go below deck because, so he said, he could not become wetter. He rode a horse till late in life.

In all that, again the influence of Suffolk comes in. It is a tough county and it does not breed weak and too gentle men. That is perhaps why Suffolk people live to a hearty old age. In Suffolk FitzGerald was comparatively young when he died at the age of seventy-four.

And speaking of toughness, I myself have witnessed a case of true toughness in Suffolk. I am not thinking of FitzGerald but of a goose called Lucia di Lammermoor. She was an exceptional goose. She had yellow-rimmed eyes and honked so loudly that it was easy to imagine that one could hear her as far as Little Bealings. She lived with two other geese in the orchard of Boulge, which is situated between church and the walled-in garden. The fate of Lucia was to be killed and eaten, but only as the last of the three geese because I was fond of her. First went the gander, a nasty fellow full of fight and hissing. Then the gardeners persuaded me that Lucia should come next, she being the fatter of the remaining two. So I compromised. Next Thursday, I said, I would be going to London. Let her, therefore, die next Thursday.

On Thursday we went to London and came back the same night. In June the nightingales sing indeed at Boulge. If the theory is correct that birds' song is a challenge to fight, then plenty of challenging goes on in June at Boulge, greatly added to by the cuckoo, the voice of which seemed to be calling from every tree in Boulge Wood, but always the same cuckoo it seemed. My wife and I went out into the grounds, since that was one of the few nights that June when it did not rain. We spoke of this, that, and the other; Lucia's name was not mentioned. She was dead. As we came into the orchard we heard a sudden loud honking that was unmistakable. I thought for a moment that Lucia's ghost was calling to my remorseful heart; but there she was in the fat flesh, delighted to see us. What happened was that the gardeners had killed the other goose by mistake.

So we decided that, as no man should hang twice, she would be pardoned and turned into a pet. The new pet next morning was taken down to the lake where, honking delightedly, she swam about with the duck and the clandestine water hens. "Dear old Lucia," I said.

65

This would make a good story; FitzGerald would have enjoyed it, what with his devotion to pigeons, duck, and parrot. It had, unfortunately, an ending typical of our age. The first day or so she was happy on the lake. Then she began to wander and she had to be chased back from the ornamental garden which, suspiciously enough, was near the orchard and her late pen. She was found, shortly after, again in the ornamental garden and this time nearer to the orchard. She was, once more, chased to the lake of liberty, but the moment one's back was turned, she retraced her waddling steps to the orchard.

Within a few days she found her way to the orchard itself and stationed herself outside the wire netting of her prison, honking merrily. Eventually she was allowed back into the pen where she settled down to be a contented prisoner for life. Next day her throat was cut, and when I arrived on the bloody scene some hours after her death, the gardener said to me, "She took a very long time dying."

That in Suffolk is a compliment, but the poor bird should have known that one cannot have it both ways.

Doctor Malkin was lame, kindly, and good humored. On Sundays the boys tripped to St. James's Church and on weekdays they sat in their schoolroom, the ceiling of which was supported by massive oak beams.

The most important aspect of FitzGerald's schooldays was the beginning of his collection of friends. Friendship, for him, as he freely admitted, was akin to love. If love, as it undoubtedly is, proves to be the great achievement of the human heart, then FitzGerald's was a triumphant heart. Among the boys at Bury the following became his lifelong friends: James Spedding, a man almost without a fault; J. M. Kemble, Fanny's brother, who became a fine Anglo-Saxon scholar; W. Bodham Donne, who was to be the first Librarian of the London Library before he was appointed Reader of Plays; and William Airy, some day Vicar of Keysoe.

Spedding and Donne were to play a major part in FitzGerald's life. Donne while at Bury boarded with one of the masters, a Rev. J. Shore, and his tutor was the Rev. Williams of Thornham. The Rev. Williams was a friend of Charles Lamb, and apparently it was on Lamb's way to visit him that, when asked by a fellow passenger about the prospect of the turnip crops, Lamb replied that he believed it depended on the number of boiled legs of mutton. That is the sort of witticism for which I dislike Lamb.

James Spedding was to become a man of great integrity, charm, brains, and good looks, notwithstanding his premature baldness, which became the target for some of FitzGerald's less funny jokes. Though he was to keep his own hair not for long, yet FitzGerald compared Spedding's dome to Mont Blanc. Spedding understood FitzGerald, he appreciated what he was: a mixture of bear and pixie. Here is an extract from a letter he wrote to Donne in 1835, summing up his schoolmate at Bury:

E.FG. was here for about a month and left us some weeks ago. He is the prince of Quietists. I reckon myself a quiet man but that is nature, in him it is principle. Half the self-sacrifice, the self-denial, the moral resolution which he exercises to keep himself easy, would amply furnish forth a martyr or a missionary. His tranquility is like a pirated copy of the peace of God. Truly he is a most comfortable companion. He would have everybody around him as tranquil as himself.

Do you know that Deville the phrenologist predicted of him that he would be given to theology and Religion in the supernatural parts? Was there ever so felicitous a mistake? Was there ever a stranger instance of the organs of marvellousness and veneration predominant, though driven so effectually out of their ordinary if not natural channel? I take this to be the secret of all that is strange and wayward in his judgment on matters of art: for very strange and wayward they appear to me, though so original and often so profound and luminous.

One can quote this letter as much to understand Spedding as FitzGerald. He, too, had a gift for friendship and a calm yet luminous brain; his feeling for the right word is as apparent as his sense of balance. He was a man of many talents. A good rural landlord, a good shot, a fine talker with the integrity of good mind and quiet soul. He could have risen to the dazzling worldly heights man generally covets. He was for a short period Under Secretary of State in the Colonial Office but that meant little to him. He gave most of his life and time to Francis Bacon. Between 1861–74 he published *Bacon's Life and Letters* in seven volumes as a supplement, if you please, to his *Bacon's Works,* also in seven volumes.

FitzGerald, who was only too aware of his own laziness, and knew he was undecided and often futile —miserable, too, when thinking of his futility—took exception to Spedding's wasting a lifetime on Bacon. Because he loved and admired his friend, it infuriated him that so much talent, work, and knowledge should be spent on Bacon, for whom he, FitzGerald, cared little. One's own life is, after all, one's own business, but a friend's life seems somehow to call for comment. When the heavy, erudite Bacon tomes began to appear, FitzGerald did not hide his impatience and disapproval. He did not conceal from Spedding his regret that he had devoted himself entirely to Bacon. "An opinion," Sir Frederic Pollock says, "which he took no pains to conceal from Spedding himself and that very naturally at last led to some estrangement on Spedding's part." It was not always easy to love FitzGerald.

In 1881 Spedding died. He had been run over by a

cab. He died as he had lived, looking at suffering and agony quietly and without rancor. FitzGerald was heartbroken. He almost forgave him Bacon.

With Bodham Donne, friendship was easy sailing. His gift for friendship was coupled with an interest in his friends' movements, thoughts, and doings. Through his letters I can follow FitzGerald's life as though I had lived with him. Donne was too good-humored even for FitzGerald in his love ever to bear him a grudge.

It is recorded that on Speech Day, in 1824, at Bury, Airy recited "Catarach" from Beaumont and Fletcher; Spedding, "Gray's Bard"; Kemble, "Alexander's Feast"; and FitzGerald, Swift's "Mr. Bickerstaff." With that one can safely say good-by to FitzGerald's schooldays. But I wish one knew more of what he did during his holidays and whether his skeptical attitude toward religion had had its seed at Bury. He was the son of the richest parents of Doctor Malkin's school, and the aloofness which lack of poverty and financial worry at home produces must have made its influence felt.

His surroundings at Bury had been exquisite. Bury is a town of charm; civilization hangs beneath the blue sky which was invariably blue whenever I visited the town. No Suffolk town I found gives that sense of quiet culture which Bury has. Suffolk is a primeval land—a sweeping statement, but FitzGerald felt the same way about it. He could have settled on any other of his mother's domains, yet he chose her Suffolk estate because he loved the raw force of nature. His devotion and friendship for fisherman John Fletcher, called Posh, was in some respect like the admiration he had for the shaking howling oaks of Boulge. However, Bury ingrained a true sense of letters which became his background too.

With Spedding, Kemble, Donne, and Airy he went up to Cambridge.

It must be admitted that the life of a man born in 1809 and living till 1883, through an age in which even the Navy, except for its military side, was run as a private enterprise, can, if the man was able to stand apart from his age, have interest for us only from the inside. Otherwise such a life easily becomes a collection of boring dates and facts. FitzGerald's life is a pile of dates, giving the length of a stay with a friend, the day he set forth on a journey, and so on. Those dates give little else to us.

And for him the historical dates of his time meant just as little. The fall of the Wellington Government or the burning of Bristol passed him by and made no difference to him. The Reform Act, the Lancashire Cotton Famine, or the Rural Housing Report of 1864 find no echo in him. On the other hand, if he did look at the world, his interest was only in the protagonists and not in the events. When Louis Philippe's reign ended his comment was: "Don't you rather rejoice at the pickle the King of France finds himself in? I don't know why but I have a sneaking dislike of the old knave. How he must pine to summon up Talleyrand's Ghost and what a Ghost it must be wherever he is!"

That, indeed, is a human approach to the events of 1848, but it was all the reaction events could produce in him. As for myself, finding my way about in the old room, I decided I would take a leaf out of Fitz-Gerald's book: I would keep my interest on the events of his life which I found of importance and let the pile of dates look after itself.

So FitzGerald is by now entered into Trinity College, Cambridge, and even at the beginning of his Cambridge days one feels that curious yet jealous aloofness which was to become his stock in trade. He was seventeen years old when he went up. He did not live in College but boarded with a Mrs. Perry at 19 King's Parade. He stayed with her throughout his University career.

He came up rather propitiously, for at Cambridge at the time were men who would become ornaments of the century. Besides, he did not arrive alone: there were his friends Donne, Spedding, and Airy. He was considered to be of retiring habits. That might be one explanation why he was not an Apostle. The Apostles' official title was The Cambridge Conversazione Society. They called themselves Apostles because their original number was twelve; but, as it happens with such original ideas, the idea slowly atrophied, and in their hearts the Apostles considered themselves to be apostles indeed. Several of them played a part in FitzGerald's life. Here, then, is their list, which also shows what excellent company there was around the young man of retired habits.

William Henry Brookfield, *later* Rector of Somerby *and* Cannon of Ealdland
Joseph Henry Blakeley, *later* Dean of Lincoln
Charles Buller, *later* M.P., Judge·Advocate, etc.
John Mitchell Kemble, *later* Examiner of Plays
Richard Monkton Milnes, *later* the first Lord Houghton
James Spedding
Henry Lushington, Chief Secretary at Malta
John Sterling
Alfred Tennyson
Arthur Henry Hallam, of *In Memoriam* fame
Richard Chenevix Trench, *later* Archbishop of Dublin
George Stovin Venables

These were the original founders. Later Donne, too, became an Apostle. FitzGerald and Tennyson did not meet at Cambridge, though FitzGerald remembered seeing him. Later they became friends, and for a lifetime FitzGerald gave him his love.

As the day for FitzGerald to meet Thackeray is now approaching, one Apostle, Brookfield, is worthy of special mention. Thackeray was in love with Brookfield's wife for years, and out of that love affair the Rector and Apostle does not come out well. For years he watched, or rather did not watch, the relationship between his wife and the fashionable novelist. Perhaps it flattered him to have the well-known man so often in his house; perhaps he even thought that through Thackeray's letters to his wife a sort of immortality would one day be his. At any rate, after years of the calm of triangular existence, Brookfield made a scene with his wife in front of Thackeray. It was an awful scene of which Thackeray's comment was: "I stabbed the husband express to put her up as high as I could to make *zusammenkunft* impossible."

The husband, only figuratively stabbed, and wife stayed nevertheless together, and sadly Thackeray ceased to be the woman's friend.

The Master of Trinity was Christopher Wordsworth, the poet's brother. It is conceivable that FitzGerald's dislike of the poet had something to do with the brother of whom he wrote, "He used to drawl out the Chapel responses so that we called him the Meeserable Sinner and his brother the Meeserable Poet."

Mr. Terhune, the latest biographer, conjures up a cheery life at Cambridge, while the Cam, so he tells one, slips coaxingly through the Backs. But FitzGerald left Cambridge an unbeliever, a man ready to shun society for good, and a vegetarian, so his time perhaps was not as cheery as the coaxing Cam might have expected. Something definitely had happened to him during his stay at Cambridge. Young men around twenty do not easily become recluses both morally and physically.

For a long time I wished I knew what had happened to him at Cambridge. I wished that the same way as I wish I knew what became of Mr. Cedar Squirrel during the big cold of '47.

Mr. Cedar Squirrel (a red squirrel, there being luckily no gray squirrels at Boulge) lived in the large cedar outside my bedroom window. He was a refined squirrel, quite different from Mr. Common Squirrel whose home was in a pine tree near the lake. Both of them received equal attention from my Dandie Dinmont terrier, Jamie. For some reason of his own Jamie hated squirrels. He was a dog of mild habits; he never hunted and if he saw a rabbit he let it be. Squirrels, however, brought out in him all the hatred and war-like spirit for which Dandies are renowned. If he caught sight of a squirrel, with gnashing teeth he hurled himself after it. The squirrel inevitably went into a tree and Jamie would try to jump after it, the jump, on account of his heavy body and short legs, not being much of a jump. The squirrel was surely amused. Now and then Jamie would sit for hours under the tree looking up, full of hope.

I for one could appreciate his dislike of Mr. Common Squirrel who was a cold and hard, bullying kind of squirrel; Mr. Cedar Squirrel was of a gentle nature. The dining room windows opened on the drive and outside the windows was a stone balustrade embracing the drive. On that balustrade Mr. Cedar Squirrel would promenade in the mornings. Then came the winter with the gray sky black with rooks and the clay soil hammered down by the continuously falling snow. If I wanted to drive to Woodbridge I had to take the gardeners in the back of the car so that they could dig the car out if the snow became too deep; and, of course, the snow did become too deep.

Then came the thaw and the spring with the sun on the meadows, but in vain we hoped for Mr. Cedar Squirrel to reappear from his tree. He was not seen again, though, needless to add, Mr. Common Squirrel was hale and hearty, even fatter than he had been in the autumn. The fate of Mr. Cedar Squirrel will remain a mystery, but the answer to FitzGerald's transformation did come to me: William Makepeace Thackeray is the answer.

In Cambridge, then, did the transformation come, for a curious transformation it undoubtedly was. At the age of twenty-one FitzGerald was already the man who was to die fifty-three years later. It is true that his crotchets, dislikes, and intolerance increased with the years, but apart from the years one can safely say that the youth who went down from Cambridge had already that hard core which many decades later would instinctively frighten the Woodbridge children when they caught sight of him. He was, in short, already the man who said to his brother John's grandson, when the little boy approached him, trembling: "Take that apple, child, and go."

My conviction is that he formed a romantic attachment to Thackeray, that in fact Thackeray was the object of his first *Schwärmerei*. (I use the German word because it is more descriptive of FitzGerald's attachments than any similar word in English.) It did not, however, work out as the then probably still romantic young man expected. Such attachments seldom work out as the dreamy young heart expects; FitzGerald was as intolerant of disillusion as of himself. An astronomer once told me that if one is capable of working with and obtaining results from an hypothesis, then it

77

cannot be altogether wrong; and my hypothesis works surprisingly well.

It is not difficult to picture FitzGerald leading the average undergraduate's life. He was not keen on games, the overwhelming influence of Mathematics left him cold; he drank as the others did, went for walks, and then probably drank more. In 1829 he engaged a private tutor, a Mr. Williams, and it was through him that he met Thackeray.

Before going further, one had better look at Thackeray and at the baggage with which he came to Cambridge. FitzGerald's baggage contained Suffolk, trees, flowers, the Deben, the sea, Bredfield House, and a rich overbearing mother. Thackeray's was of a different kind, with the exception of the mother, for Mrs. Carmichael-Smyth was as overbearing as Mary Frances, though far from rich.

Thackeray was born in Calcutta in 1811 and, when he was four years old, his father, Richmond Thackeray, died. Two years later his mother sent him to England and in the same year she married an Engineer Officer, Captain Henry Carmichael-Smyth, with whom she returned to England. Thackeray went to Charterhouse School in London and thence to Trinity. He was gay, glib, and facetious, the kind of person who would make a deep impression on a retiring quietist like FitzGerald.

Thackeray's relationship with his mother was one of deep love. He stood up against her only when she tried to influence his daughters in matters of religion. She had come under the rule, as it were, of French Calvinists. That influence Thackeray resented, but otherwise it was pure devotion.

"Your rebuke," he would write to her, "is not a just one, my dear Mother, as to my only half reading your letters. I have looked over the letter and you do not mention the day of your departure from Weymouth. . . ."

His mother went on loving and rebuking him, even when famous, even when deep in middle age.

His friendship with FitzGerald had a gay and noisy beginning. Thackeray liked to sing the "Friars of Orders Grey" and FitzGerald listened adoringly. The memory of these times persisted, for we find Fitz-Gerald writing to Anne Thackeray in December 1876, twelve years after her father's death:

Dear Annie Thackeray,

Messrs. Smith and Elder very politely gave me leave to print, and may be publish, three Stanzas of your Father's "Ho, pretty Page," adapted (under proper direction) to an old Cambridge Tune, which he and I have sung together, tho' not to these fine Words, as you may guess. I asked this of Messrs. Smith and Elder, because I thought they had the Copyright. But I did not mean to publish them unless with your Approval: only to print a few Copies for friends. And I will stop even that, if you don't choose. Please to tell me in half a dozen words as directly as you can.

The Words, you know, are so delightful (stanzas one, two, and the last), and the old Tune of "Troll, troll, the bonny brown Bowl" so pretty, and (with some addition) so appropriate, I think, that I fancied others beside Friends might like to have them together. But, if you don't approve, the whole thing shall be quashed. Which I ought to have asked before: but I thought your Publishers' sanction might include yours. Please, I say, to say Yes or No as soon as you can.

And a little later, in February 1877, he wrote to one of the recipients of the printed song, C. E. Newton:

I really only write now to prevent your doing so in ac-knowledgment of Thackeray's Song which I sent you, and you perhaps knew the handwriting of the Address. Pray don't write about such a thing, so soon after the very kind Letter I have just had from you. Why I sent you the Song I can hardly tell, not knowing if you care for Thackeray or Music; but that must be as it is; only, do not, pray, write expressly about it. The Song is what it pretends to be: the words speak for themselves; very beautiful, I think: the Tune is one which Thackeray and I knew at College, belonging to some rather free Cavalier words,

Troll, troll, the bonny brown Bowl,

with four bars interpolated to let in the Page. I have so sung it (without a Voice to myself these dozen years, since his Death, and so I have got the words decently arranged, in case others should like them as well as myself. *Voilà tout!* . . .

Though Thackeray was the keener cartoonist of the two, in one of FitzGerald's scrapbooks there is a drawing he made of Thackeray; from the artist's point of view FitzGerald did not by a long chalk possess the facile talent for drawing of his friend. One imagines FitzGerald wanted to join in everything Thackeray did. He wished to be as jolly and facetious as his friend was. For Thackeray Cambridge was a roisterous period; but the trouble with Thackeray was that he tried to turn all periods into one big slice of roistering. True he could be sad, disillusioned, and heavy with worry; in praise of him it must be said that he at least did his best to hide that side of his nature, notwithstanding that he lived in an age of copious tears. At Cambridge, however, there was as yet no cause for sadness. It was all gaiety. FitzGerald called Thackeray "Old Thack," and being the older of the two, was flattered by being called "Yedward" and "Teddibus."

They both belonged to a debating club and W. H. Thompson, later Master of Trinity, relates that Thackeray at Cambridge led a lazy but pleasant gentleman-like life. No doubt, he says, he had much literary talk with FitzGerald, but not on University subjects. Thackeray drank a lot.

"I have," he informed his mother, "just left three

drunken men whom I had much ado to pacify. I don't know the reason but I now (although I have only drunk two glasses of wine this day & that at 4 o'clock) feel half drunk myself."

It is an amusing conjecture that the three drunken men were his three great friends: Allen, later Archdeacon; Groome, later Archdeacon, too; and Fitz-Gerald.

Archdeacon Allen recorded in his diary that one day Thackeray came to him and that they had a serious conversation in the course of which Thackeray burst into tears and, moved by his own tears, decided to lead a new life, which of course he never did. After all, that is perhaps what new lives are for. But it was not only Thackeray who was in tears that day: Allen and FitzGerald cried, too, and, glistening with tears, prayed for Thackeray. So, one notes, FitzGerald still prayed in those Cambridge days.

It is feasible that the company of Thackeray was the cause of a row between Mary Frances and her son. Anyway they made it up and FitzGerald was left to enjoy Thackeray's company.

The final examination began June 15, 1830. Fitz-Gerald received his degree though he had not done well with Paley's *Evidences*. He went off to Paris to stay with a Purcell aunt, and soon there Thackeray joined him. That Thackeray had no business to do; he was expected by his mother to be elsewhere. Their stay in Paris was the culminating point of FitzGerald's idolizing of Old Thack. A year later when he wrote to him, "I see few people I care about, and so, oh, Willy, be constant to me," it was already the voice of a man halfway down the slope of disillusion.

Thackeray spent one more term at Cambridge and then left without taking a degree. It would have been more logical had it been the other way round, but it should not be forgotten that he was two years younger than FitzGerald. And now the question is: what did that deep love and adoration leave behind?

It is a fact that their friendship lasted till Thackeray's death, and even longer, since FitzGerald left to Thackeray's eldest daughter the sum of five hundred pounds in his will; but the actual result of that high wind of love can be found in a letter FitzGerald wrote to Allen, saying that he would become a great bear having many Utopian ideas about society. The Utopian ideas were simply to shun society altogether, and one must admit he succeeded completely.

For FitzGerald by then was a disillusioned man. After all, Thackeray could not give him those high qualities of mind and soul which the infatuated youth demanded from his idol. Not only in youth, but, unfortunately for him, throughout life, FitzGerald strove for perfection. His friends must be perfect, other people's writings must be perfect, and even his own. Hence the many rewritings and fears of publication. Already at Cambridge, but in Paris quite certainly, he must have noticed the seamy side of Thackeray's character. Though Thackeray had a great heart, was kind and generous, he was a snob of the first order. He could not resist the company of the rich and the titled. He ran after them, flattered them, fawned on them. Today in London there are, knocking about, letters of Thackeray which find no buyers for the reason that they are a monotonous row of acceptances of invitations to dine with the titled and the rich.

That vein of snobbism is a harmless if naïve one. One smiles at the snob or pities him, but FitzGerald had not the gift of the patient smile.

When Thackeray left Cambridge for his home at Weymouth, FitzGerald refused to go to see him. There was a grain of charming, though now and then irritating, pouting in all FitzGerald's loves and friendships. No, he would not go and see his friend; yes, the friend must be with him and nobody else. He was then as he was to be in many years to come when he and Posh were walking along the pier at Lowestoft. A man came up to Posh and there they stood for a while talking of wind, fish, tide, and similar topics. FitzGerald suddenly took Posh by the arm and pulled him away saying, "This is my guest." Posh's comment afterwards was: "He made me look a complete cake."

The FitzGerald of Posh's days was not much different from the FitzGerald who would not visit Thackeray. But it was not easy to get Thackeray out of his mind. He was at Geldestone, Thackeray at Weymouth; the evening came with that loneliness and longing which invariably prompted FitzGerald to take pen to paper. A long letter followed full of love and recriminations: "Now Thackeray I lay you ten thousand pounds that you will be thoroughly disappointed when we come together— our letters have been so warm that we shall expect each minute to contain a sentence like those in our letters."

He goes on to suggest that they had better not meet. It would not be the same as it had been in London and Cambridge. It is seven in the evening, the appropriate hour for such a letter. He assures Thackeray he is not speaking in a lighthearted vein. His sister, with whom he is staying, is in the drawing room, he in his room ready to spin a yarn with his Willy. The anger and disappointment begin to fade and he chats away about Pope, Hume, Byron, Helvetius, Diderot, and Shakespeare. He sees himself that his anger has gone: "What have I been doing the last hour? Behold these verses, they are the fruits; for they never came into my head before: but the wind was blowing hard at the window & I somehow began to think of Will Thackeray: so the cockles of my heart were warmed, and up sprouts the following: I have drunk a glass of port & sit down to transcribe them."

One cannot but notice here a curious trait of Fitz-Gerald, namely the self-sufficiency of his longing. Usually one tries to make an effort to end the loneliness of longing. It was not so with him. Distance was part and parcel of his love. Alone in his bedroom, after a glass of port, he was happy with his longing for Thackeray. It was complete on account of the very distance that separated them. Pen and paper were as good a medium of contact as an arm round the shoulder. One is alone with the friend, so alone that not even his presence could jar.

The caravan which started for the Dawn of Nothing was preferable to the caravan which might have taken him from Ispahan to Khorassan.

The verses which I reproduce are not good verses, but they prove how he could let himself go when thus completely alone with his friend:

I

I cared not for life: for true friend I had none
I had heard 'twas a blessing not under the sun:
Some figures called friends, hollow, proud or cold-hearted
Came to me like shadows—like shadows departed:

86

But a day came that turned all my sorrows to glee
When I first saw Willy, and Willy saw me!

2

The thought of my Willy is always a cheerer;
My wine has new flavour—the fire burns clearer:
The sun ever shines—I am pleased with all things;—
And this crazy old world seems to go with new springs;—
And when we're together, (Oh! soon may it be!)
The world may go kissing of comets for me!

3

The chair that Will sat in, I sit in the best;
The tobacco is sweetest which Willy hath blest;
And I never found out that my wine tasted ill
When a tear would drop in it, for thinking of Will.

There are three more verses in a similar vein. "These are my verses," commented FitzGerald. "I have polished them a little more which has not done them any good." Nevertheless, they were sent off to Will, who, at times, when socially not much engaged, could also feel for his Teddibus.

"Good bye now dear FitzGerald," he once wrote. "Write me a letter soon, for the warm weather is coming & I am growing romantick—God bless you."

He could be more matter of fact: "Now I have been making myself a glass of punch & here is your health

87

God bless you my dear old boy & may you & I drink many glasses of punch together."

By the time *Vanity Fair* appeared, the friendship had turned into a smooth but distant one. FitzGerald was in Suffolk, Thackeray in London. FitzGerald would spend his evenings alone or in the company of parson, farmer, solicitor, and bank clerk, whereas his Will feverishly allowed himself to be lionized. Having said that the Englishman dearly loves a lord, Thackeray loved lords as dearly as any of his fellow countrymen could. FitzGerald, on the other hand, did not care for lords. He was completely bereft of snobbery, at least of the extrovert sort. Perhaps it was introvert snobbery that he often preferred the company of his social inferiors. He could more dominate, more keep to himself men who were not his equals.

There is the well-known story of a man (no name given) boasting of dukes and marquises he knew. Fitz-Gerald became tired of his talk, rose, lighted a candle, went to the door, stopped, his countenance turned sad, and in a sad voice said, "I once knew a lord, too, but he is dead."

Could Thackeray have been the man who boasted of his Peers? If so, the sadness of tone and features was heartbreakingly real and then this story should not go down as one of FitzGerald's jokes.

The years followed each other; the friendship remained, with the distance growing. In 1848 Thackeray, in one of his countless letters to Mrs. Brookfield, said, "I went to see dear old FitzGerald yesterday. I have cared for him tenderly and with a noble affection for twenty years. When we first became friends I had not learnt to love a woman."

FitzGerald never truly had, but if he thought of Mrs. Thackeray and Mrs. Brookfield he could not have felt that he had missed much.

It is surprising yet characteristic of FitzGerald that he refused to admit or understand that underneath the huge social lion's mane there were often qualms, and also the gift to despise himself. It was not to Fitz-Gerald (probably he was too proud to do so) but to Mrs. Sartoris that Thackeray wrote: "The other day somebody in Harley Street with whom I couldn't dine because I promised them at home said, 'You won't come because we haven't got a Lord.'"

FitzGerald would have been delighted and moved if his friend had written that self-abasing letter to him. He refused to admit that Thackeray was not wholly the lion. He told Frederic Tennyson, the poet's brother, that Thackeray moved in such a great world that he was afraid of him and that Thackeray and he were content to regard each other at a distance. The distance, however, was mostly of FitzGerald's making.

Oh, if Willy had remained with him for always, always—alone with him and completely with him. Yet in 1851 he went to stay with Thackeray. He was not, with his jealousy, frustration, and love, an easy guest to look after. Bears should not embrace too hard, and FitzGerald's trouble and charm were that he would take into his huge grip those he loved.

Thackeray wrote of that visit to his mother to say that Old Fitz was there staying for a day or two. He wished it might be for a month or two. "We are young fellows when we meet: and I am not spoiled for him." Undoubtedly if in the beginning FitzGerald wanted more than Thackeray could give, one cannot blame Thackeray for that. FitzGerald's heart was a complicated affair. It could rejoice with Thackeray, who, because he was a fundamentally worried man, rejoiced all the time, but then FitzGerald's heart had to lacerate itself. Suddenly one day in 1852 he burned Thackeray's letters, letters he had cherished a lot. As the letters burned, so the flames in the shape of a knife must have stabbed deep into his heart. He wrote from Boulge the following explanation:

My dear old Thackeray,

I have been looking over a heap of your letters—from the first in 1831 to the last of some months back—and what do you think I have done with the greater part?—why burnt them!—with great remorse, I assure you; but I had two good reasons—first I am rather *ashamed* (and nothing else) of your repeated, and magnanimously blind over-estimate of myself; and secondly I thought that if I were to die before setting my house in order those letters might fall into unwise hands, and perhaps (now you are become famous) get published according to the vile fashion of the day.

But I have cut out and preserved many parts of these letters, which you shall see when you come to spend those celebrated "two days" here which I really do want you to come and spend some time in the summer. You laugh at *time* I specify: but I assure you it is on your account I do so—you would be very weary of more on many accounts. I will make no Lion of you. . . .

The dig about the lion was for FitzGerald irresistible. But the burning of the letters is of more interest. I used to know a lady who wrote fourteen novels of sorts a year, under several different names. Those novels were all about love, of the simple, heart-warming, uncomplicated variety. Her men were handsome, clean, and good; her women were beautiful, clean, and good; love was in everybody's eyes. The lady managed to educate on her earnings three strapping children. She confided in me one day that when she did not know how to pad the middle of a novel and the course of smooth love would end the book with sixty-five thousand words in lieu of the seventy-five thousand stipulated by the publisher, she invariably made the hero tear up the photograph of the heroine, thus giving herself respite. Besides, she added, tearing up the photograph of the beloved was true romance. FitzGerald was a romantic, too.

In the same letter he told Thackeray that he was making his will and would leave five hundred pounds to each of Thackeray's daughters. If Thackeray died first, he would look after them. The letter ends with these words: "Goodbye my dearest old Thackeray. As I get older I don't get colder, I believe: which is lucky you will think." Dining with Lady Molesworth or the Rothschilds, Thackeray must have considered that lucky too.

The contrast of their lives was immense. Success and the urbanity of polite London on one side and the howling winds of Boulge on the other. "But goodbye, goodbye, my dear Old Thackeray," FitzGerald would cry, "& believe (for I can assert) that I am while I live yrs ever." But somehow it never is good-by. He wants Thackeray's portrait, he must write on, for it is such a comfort to talk to Will, even if one has to leave unsmoked half the cigar one was burning to his memory. "My dear Thackeray I wonder if this sentimentality bores you!" It was easy to ask that as by then the distance between them was truly great: Thackeray was in America.

Thackeray was now a sick man fighting hard with American trips and lectures in order to find enough money to leave his daughters comfortably off. That, indeed, was admirable, and indeed it was a comfort to know that his old Teddibus would stand by his daughters in the event of his death. His own great gusto was dying. It would not take him long to follow.

"Isn't it better," he asked, but not from FitzGerald, "to blow the light out than sit among the broken meats and collapsed jellies and vapid heeltaps?"

Had he put that question to FitzGerald, FitzGerald would have cried over it, kissed the paper, and the barrier he had built up between Old Thack and himself would have collapsed. Alas, one seldom puts the question to the person who might not only have the right answer but the gift to enjoy the question.

Thackeray's life was reaching its end, and even a few hard inches from the grave he was unaware that he was in an indirect manner one of the inspirers of the Rubáiyát. Yet he was, for the early FitzGerald was driven by him into the cave of the crotchety recluse. It was the recluse, grumpy and dissatisfied with his beloved Will, who one day began to dream of the sensual shapes of the East while the wind whipped the German Ocean.

In 1863 Thackeray died. His light did not quite go out, for FitzGerald carried it till his own went out too. Probably he never knew that when Anne Thackeray asked her father who had been his best-beloved friend, Thackeray answered, "There was Old Fitz, and I was very fond of Brookfield once." Then after a short silence, still thinking of Brookfield, he added, "We shall be very good friends in hell together." That, of course, sounds quite possible, provided Mrs. Brookfield went elsewhere.

But in the old room there is still the FitzGerald just down from Cambridge, at the end of the Paris trip. He and Thackeray parted in Paris—Thackeray to go off to Germany, FitzGerald to start on the lonely road that led to the Rubáiyát. FitzGerald arrived back at Southampton. John Allen was in the vicinity and, having heard that FitzGerald had arrived, went to see him. He had already gone to bed: with a broken heart one often goes early to bed. The next morning Allen saw him. FitzGerald was almost in tears and Allen thought what an affectionate fellow he was. The tears must have poured fast when a little later a letter came from Thackeray. It contained a drawing of himself in breeches and cocked hat, both of which he wore when he was introduced at Weimar to the Grand Duke.

Shortly after, FitzGerald took to vegetarianism.

Part Three

MY STUDY at Boulge faced west. The afternoon sun could be so glaring in the hot summer of '47 that my only vista was the dark blue roller blind before me; but when the sun began to sink behind Horse Covert, I let up the blind, and then before me was the early evening life of Boulge, a life that had not much changed since FitzGerald's days. Out in the field which mounted slowly toward Boulge Wood were two of Mr. Anderson's Suffolk Punches with their two foals. A little earlier the mares had still been in the shade of a tree, but now in the cool of the oncoming evening the foals frolicked and the mares quietly trotted after them.

The departing light was on the lake, and the second gardener was throwing pebbles and earth at two wayward duck which were not in the mood to go into the pen. The light was, too, on the oats on the other side of the railing, and the oats of '47 looked and were healthier than the oats of the year before when storms and rain had flattened them.

Nearer to, life was truly busy. A rabbit sat between two rows of trees, and behind the rabbit sat another. From a clump of bushes on the right a hen pheasant emerged; not far behind her came an old cock. The light, which was rapidly fading and could just break through the trees of Horse Covert, kissed the cock's plumage. The kisses were like the crosses lovesick girls put at the end of their letters. In a wide circle around cock and hen the grass was lively: that circle consisted of growing pheasant chicks. They passed the rabbits, unseeing and unnoticed—which is a curious characteristic of the wild life of fields and woods. Unless they meet an enemy or partner for mating, all seem impervious to one another. I have seen pheasants among rooks, and the rooks appeared as unaware of the pheasants' existence as the pheasants were of theirs.

In the distance sheep bleated, and the sounds of a tractor persisted till night fell. A blackbird sang and, much later, when there was silence and neither nightingale nor the sometimes boring cuckoo could longer be heard, the owls began to hoot, and in the darkness, like twisted dead souls, flew the bats. Of bats at Boulge there were thousands. Jamie, the Dandie, stood in the garden having one of his barking sessions. Then, to bed, and in the bedroom was a bat flying round in uneasy circles.

The scene changes. It is the rainy autumn of '46 and from my study's window I saw the glory of the rotting golden leaves which in that rainy autumn somehow refused to come down. My mind was still busy with the day before, the first pheasant shoot of the season. For me shooting is almost a vice. To stand outside a wood waiting for the beaters to come down is perhaps my dearest moment. The sky on that day was blue though it had rained hard the night before. The leaves were still dripping. The quick succession of knocking sounds was like a half-circle before me: the beaters were coming down. Knock-knock, and you heard an old cock rise; the beaters shouted but the clever old bird flew off in the opposite direction. A rabbit appeared at the edge of the wood, sat down, and listened. The gun on my right shot it. Then in front of me I heard careful footsteps and the footsteps turned into a clatter of wings: a low hen pheasant flew off to the right. I missed it.

Knock-knock, came the beaters, and then, beautifully, another knock-knock began. A little bit behind me was a hollow tree, the sort of tree jackdaws patronize. But now it was a woodpecker which had come to give some helping knocks to the beaters. It was a fine space of time, with the beaters in front and the woodpecker, like the fairy's echo, behind. "Cock to the right," and noisy and proud, out flew a cock pheasant and up there in the sun I killed it. Undisturbed, the woodpecker continued to beat for us.

That was the autumn which turned into a mild winter, or so it seemed, till winter decided to become a wild, raging, white beast. The wind came to help it and the low clouds shielded it. Birds died by the thousand. The morsels of bread one threw into the snow were of but small help. The birds, poor things, came, and my miserable dogs, overfed and overbearing, would go out into the snow and spend hours sniffing for bread crumbs. One evening my wife found a half-frozen green woodpecker with a broken wing. She put it for the night, with bread crumbs and milk, into the airing cupboard. In the morning the woodpecker was dead. Wild duck, which seldom visited us, came to the frozen pond.

Spring refused to come. One had visions of the snow staying through the summer waiting for reinforcements from next winter. One day driving, or rather skidding, to Ipswich, I imagined I saw sign of thaw. Here a drip, there something almost akin to a puddle; but in the afternoon the world began to freeze again. When at long last the spring arrived, primroses were already on the way. In a month's time the yellow glory of daffodils followed.

With the cycle of the seasons and the years so well before my eyes, I naturally think of FitzGerald's "Meadows of Spring," which, for me, is the picture of the year surrounding Boulge like a moat.

THE MEADOWS OF SPRING

'Tis a dull sight
To see the year dying,
When winter winds
Set the yellow wood sighing:
Sighing, o! sighing.

When such a time cometh,
I do retire
Into an old room
Beside a bright fire:
Oh, pile a bright fire!

And there I sit
Reading old things,
Of knights and lorn damsels
While the wind sings—
Oh, drearily sings!

I never look out
Nor attend to the blast;
For all to be seen
Is the leaves falling fast:
Falling, falling!

99

But close at the hearth,
  Like a cricket sit I,
Reading of summer
  And chivalry—
Gallant chivalry!

Then with an old friend
  I talk of our youth—
How 'twas gladsome, but often
  Foolish, forsooth:
But gladsome, gladsome!

Or to get merry
  We sing some old rhyme,
That made the wood ring again
  In summer time!
Sweet summer time!

Then we go to smoking,
  Silent and snug:
Nought passes between us,
  Save a brown jug—
Sometimes!

And sometimes a tear
  Will rise in each eye,
Seeing the two old friends
  So merrily—
So merrily!

And ere to bed
    Go we, go we
Down on the ashes
    We kneel on the knee,
Praying together!

Thus, then live I,
    Till 'mid all the gloom,
By Heaven! the bold sun
    Is with us in the room
Shining, shining!

Then the clouds part,
    Swallows soaring between;
The spring is alive
And the meadows are green!

I jump up, like mad,
    Break the old pipe in twain,
And away to the meadows,
The meadows again!

The youthful charm of it is somewhat counterbalanced by the sadness of distance and past. It was written by a young man of .twenty-two. The skill is praiseworthy, the lyrical quality excellent, and the fifth line is an echo, delicate yet powerful. But it was not written at Boulge. In fact FitzGerald had not yet lived at Boulge at all.

It appeared in *Hone's Year Book* on April 30, 1831. Charles Lamb was moved by it, for he was of the opinion that he too could have done something like that. FitzGerald said of the poem: "These verses are in the old style; rather homely in expression: but I honestly profess to stick more to the simplicity of the old poets rather than the moderns, & to love the philosophical good humour of our old writers more than the sickly melancholy of the Byronian wits. If my verses be not good, they are good humoured & that is something."

These words are quite revealing. FitzGerald honestly believed he was conservative and that he, in every respect, conformed to the rules of the old order. (I have seen drunks pointing at slightly tipsy people, pointing with indignation, and shocked by the alcohol others have consumed.) The man who, as it were, invented the quatrain and made it almost inimitable (*vide* Swinburne's *Lau Veneris*) believed himself to be orthodox and a traditionalist. And the words quoted above also show his intolerance and at times faulty literary judgment. At twenty-two one is often intolerant, but though in many respects he aged prematurely, he remained young where intolerance was concerned. In fact, he became younger in that respect as the years whisked by. His unreasonable dislike of Mrs. Browning and his cruel words when she died would be unpardonable had Browning not written tasteless, undignified verses about FitzGerald.

It will remain for me a cause for regret that "Meadows of Spring" was written neither at nor on Boulge. Even the original of the tenth stanza, which was later rewritten, seems to stand for Boulge, wafted on the buffeted winter wind.

So winter passeth
Like a long sleep
From falling autumn
To primrose peep.

The poem was written at Naseby, which was one of Mary Frances's estates. FitzGerald's parents had an obelisk erected on the site of the battle of Naseby, but unfortunately the battle had taken place two miles away. It was the battlefield and the obelisk which brought FitzGerald and Carlyle together, for Carlyle was then much interested in Cromwell, another man of iron fist to add to his collection of idols.

At Naseby FitzGerald considered himself quite a king, and went to church in a loud blue surtout. And this is precisely where, for a moment, I must call a halt. I said in the preface that I did not wish to write a life of FitzGerald and to that I intend to stick. Otherwise this book would become a monotonous, rambling chronicle of journeys to London, Suffolk, Norfolk,

Bedfordshire, and the like; and amidst all those comings and goings FitzGerald would disappear altogether. It is of great attraction to try to report on every movement, every activity of a person one has well-nigh come to live with; but will it bring him nearer? I for one do not think so, and because of my doubt I am still in bed at Boulge, listening to the lugubrious chimes of Old Nelly.

The chimes stopped, the silence of the grave was undisturbed, but I had already taken a few steps in the old room. His origin, his childhood, Bury, Cambridge, and Thackeray, too, were behind me. A certain picture had begun to emerge; a few more details were waiting to be added to the youthful portrait. One came to mind. While still at Cambridge FitzGerald made a wager with J. Y. de Massingie. It had something to do with Bacon's marriage and was for one pound, which FitzGerald won but refused to take. Massingie insisted, so FitzGerald eventually accepted the pound, but at once bought a copy of Wordsworth's poems and presented it to Massingie. That wager was in my mind while Old Nelly chimed seven.

It seems rather surprising to us today that Mary Frances did not insist on her sons' taking up any profession. She married her daughters off, mostly to clergymen, but she let her sons go their way, which they did, John by becoming an amateur evangelist,

Peter by marrying his housekeeper and turning Roman Catholic, and Edward by moving, unnoticed even by himself, to immortality. But the first ten years after Cambridge were just years of moving about, reading, writing letters, and loving William Kenworthy Browne.

His circle of friends became like a ring around him. The wider circle was: Alfred Tennyson, whose 1832 poems FitzGerald greatly admired; Frederic Tennyson, who contributed to *Poems by Two Brothers* (perhaps it was he who made the revealing remark: "I am the gloomiest of the three brothers"); W. B. Donne; John Allen; Thackeray—of course; Robert Hinde Groome; Spedding; and Monkton Milnes. Also Carlyle. The inner circle was made up of his Suffolk cronies: George Crabbe, Vicar of Bredfield (son of the poet George Crabbe and father of the George Crabbe in whose vicarage, Merton in Norfolk, FitzGerald was to die); Bernard Barton; Thomas Churchyard; and Alfred Smith. He moved within these two circles, visited his sisters, and when there was nothing better to do, might be found wearing a raincoat outside a public house in Beccles. He read voraciously, collected pictures, and believed he knew more about them than was the case. Generally speaking, but for the shadow of his mother, his was a life of ease and of few worries.

Then Mrs. Short died. Pure tenacity and probably

the desire to hold the FitzGeralds at bay as long as possible had kept the cantankerous old wife alive; but once dead, the FitzGeralds moved to the Hall.

His biographers attach much importance to Fitz-Gerald's attitude to religion, which, more or less, crystallized itself soon after he came down from Cambridge. Doubting Castle rose and to many appears to have engulfed him. But that was not the case. Firstly, he was not alone with his doubts concerning the Established Church. For example, Donne left Cambridge without taking his degree because his conscience at the time would not let him sign the XXXIX Articles. The advance of science loosened the ties of religion, and now and then these ties snapped altogether. It was an age in which everything seemed to be marching toward its logical conclusion—the conclusion being happiness for all, plenty for all, with a material millennium inevitably ahead. Moreover, the century before had not helped to add luster to the Church of England.

FitzGerald's doubts were not based on all that. They were the doubts of the sensitive man, the qualms of the poet. But he was not consistent with his doubts, and here and there would forget them. Writing to Carlyle on the Puseyites, he could become eloquently orthodox. An intelligent man, if he is not a fanatic, is bound to be riddled with contradictions. FitzGerald was no exception. He entirely lacked fanaticism, and if he was an agnostic, then he was an exceptionally lazy one.

His inconsistency about church attendance would give a headache to a scrupulous biographer. Some eye-witnesses say he did not go to church; others insist he did. An old man, who is recently dead, told me in Woodbridge that he could remember Mr. FitzGerald sitting during Sunday service in the Church of St. George, just there under the window, his shawl on his shoulder, humming to himself.

His brother John's curious evangelism might have frightened him from an ostentatious professing of faith. His esthetic sense also intruded, but without anger, as a letter of his to Aldis Wright in 1871 testifies:

. . . I send you a shabby cheque for the Chapel: fixing on the Revd. Sinker for a precedent: below whom contributions cannot fall. He may have the excuse of an inexhaustible family which I have not. But I doubt still if you will improve your Chapel by renewing it—with Memorial Windows etc. In these days of Restoration, I like even shabby Antiquity best. I suppose the Chapel is now much as it was in Bentley's days (West Altar piece excepted) & so I should have been content to keep it. If all the Subscribers held to me & Sinker there would be no danger of tawdriness. . . .

He could speak from bitter experience. The church of Boulge is the Church of St. Michael and All the Angels. Cromwell somehow by-passed the church and, when the FitzGeralds came to Boulge, the ceiling was still of a fine blue sprinkled with golden stars and the roof was held by carved angels. John, in his evangelical impatience and, as he put it, in pious memory of his mother, renovated the church. Gone were the sky, the stars, and the carved angels. Today the ceiling of the church reminds one of those new, cold and unfeeling public houses one finds in ribbon-built areas.

It could be said that, though he did not turn his back on religion, he was as impatient of certain outward appearances of religion as of many social graces. Yet he could implore Carlyle not to despise the Hebrew rags, for the old creed was commendably effective on the generals and counselors whom Carlyle admired. He then suggested that it was well worth Carlyle's while to suffer some absurdities in the form if the spirit did well upon the whole.

It gives one pleasure that FitzGerald was never taken in by Carlyle's worship of strong brutal men, his hatred of gentle France, and love of heavy Germany. True, they were friends till the end, but it is true too that Carlyle often irritated him. In 1848 his patience had practically reached breaking point. He saw Carlyle one day, and two days later he recorded

108

that Carlyle was so gloomy and destructive that he became quite impatient with him. "I really know not if I can stand another visit without telling him so. But," he adds in that letter to Cowell, "on that we will confabulate."

It is doubtful whether he told Carlyle because he could hardly ever bring himself to be cruel to a friend. It should, however, be added that he could be quite chatty about friends behind their backs. Anyway, the friendship with Carlyle, like many other friendships, flourished at a distance, and here is a letter old Fitz-Gerald wrote to old Carlyle in 1874:

As I was told these were well-fed Pheasants from a Squire near here, I have sent you a Brace. And I only write to prevent your Niece having the trouble to acknowledge them *unless they don't reach you* by the end of this week or the Beginning of the next. I shall know that you thank one more than enough & I hope you will be able to *digest* them. Ask that Digestion! Near twenty years ago you told me you had scarcely digested anything but *Water* for some 30 years before that. Laugh at this & it will help the Pheasant down—Breadsauce & all.

A little Niece of mine once said that her Papa was gone out to shoot "Pheasants & Breadsauce."

I rejoice in what you say of Spedding's work, which will console him (if he wants that) for the Apathy of the World at large. I believe I admire his work as much, if not so wisely, as you do: but I still think Spedding might have done much more with the 40 years of Life he has employed upon it. The 40 or 50 years he writes about so admirably, were not very critical ones in English History, were they? And, as for Bacon, who, it appears, had not much influence on his times, Spedding surely leaves him where he was in the eyes of sensible & dispassionate People: no great Criminal, but no better than the Policeman of his Day: I think so far worse, in being more cowardly.

But all *this* won't help your Digestion, which I do wish to work well, and remain yours always truly

E.FG.

The pheasants were despatched and Carlyle kept FitzGerald to the letter, that is to say, he did not acknowledge the pheasants, which was less work. But that was not exactly what FitzGerald wanted. He had a sly, almost coquettish approach to his friends; they completely belonged to him and should write even if he told them not to. A little later another letter was sent to Carlyle: "I was going to write one line to Mrs. Aitken to ask her to write 'Yes' or 'No' on the enclosed card: just to signify me whether a Brace of Pheasants sent off ten days ago has yet come to hand. You know (I hope) I don't want thanks: but if my Birds missed their way, the Rail must hear of it. . . ."

That is entirely charming: the sixty-six-year-old man floundering in his own instructions. Of course Carlyle should not acknowledge the brace of birds, of course he did not want thanks, but it would be so heart-warming if the birds were acknowledged and thanks offered for them.

I have, as most of us, looked at statues of the famous and said to myself, provided I bothered to say anything, here is the statue of a famous man. The one-sided correspondence about the pheasants, however, made me truly enjoy the old room, and the distance of the years ceased to be a distance, whereas statues but add to it. Still, all that has little to do with religion and church attendance.

Whether he disliked the Established Church or not is a matter of opinion on which even his friends differed, though quite a few of them were clerics. Archdeacon Groome, for example, said, after FitzGerald's death, that because he had once been upbraided for nonattendance by the Rector of Woodbridge, Fitz-Gerald seldom if ever went to church again. Then how could my eyewitness have seen him?

The trouble is that eyewitnesses have some imagination, too, and with the passing of the years the eye weakens but imagination gathers speed. In Wood-bridge I knew a garage keeper whose mother, now long dead, had been a washerwoman at Bredfield around the time FitzGerald lived at Boulge Cottage. He told me that it often happened that FitzGerald would order a carriage to take him to Woodbridge. The carriage would arrive, wait at the door. FitzGerald in the meantime forgot about the carriage, sallied out through the back door, and went on foot to Woodbridge.

I enjoyed the tale till I heard elsewhere precisely the same story about his brother John, of whose religious convictions and church and chapel attendance one need have no doubts. John, in Boulge Church, would become so enwrapped by the sermon that he would start undressing straightaway. He wore long black gaiters and, as the sermon progressed, the gaiters were unbuttoned, taken off, the boots followed and were put in front of him; eventually he began to throw things about—chiefly candle grease from the standards holding the tapers at the end of each pew.

And thinking of John, whose eccentricities eyewitnesses and posterity liked to lay at Edward's feet, I went downstairs to the library. When John died his coffin lay for two days in this room and his blind companion, Miss Thornton, played the harmonium day and night, singing religious songs. Somehow or other, nothing of John seemed to linger in the library, which, since his time, had been redecorated in what I would call Later Abbotsford style. I picked up a baby rabbit which Celia the cat had brought in.

In a writer of the first order, Edward FitzGerald, to whom we owe the immortal and highly individualized version of

Omar Khayyám, it is easy to trace an element of homosexuality, though it appears never to have reached full and conscious development. FitzGerald was an eccentric person who, though rich and on friendly terms with some of the most distinguished men of his time, was always out of harmony with his environment. He felt himself called on to marry, very unhappily, a woman he had never been in love with and with whom he had nothing in common. All his affections were for his male friends. In early life he was devoted to his friend W. K. Browne, whom he glorified in *Euphranor*. To him Browne was at once Jonathan, Gamaliel, Apollo—the friend, the master, the God—there was scarcely a limit to his devotion and admiration. On Browne's premature death FitzGerald's heart was empty.

Thus wrote Havelock Ellis. FitzGerald's biographers, either with a genteel bit of insinuation or with downcast eyes, elude the matter. Because I wish to be honest both with FitzGerald and myself I cannot run away from what Havelock Ellis has said and what FitzGerald's life and relationships prove, too. The question then is: was he truly a homosexual? That is to say, a practicing one. I believe he was not, but he was a homosexual from the purely mental and emotional angle. I believe also—though only my acquaintance, or rather friendship, with the subject is my chief evidence—that FitzGerald never had any sexual relationship either with man or woman. There is little surprising about that. The philosophers Locke and

Kant went through life as virgins. If, however, in Fitz-Gerald's age, in which more substantial things mattered more, he could have chosen, he would have chosen man and not woman.

I do not imply that he was impotent, but he lived in a sense in an impotent age. His mother overshadowed his youth; Thackeray, his first love, disillusioned him, and he either chose or drifted into a life that was sexless. Sex, nowadays, by most people is taken for granted, and so they forget that nothing in life can be taken for granted. Sex, like many other things, is a frame of mind—or a road on which, now and then quite inadvertently, one finds oneself. FitzGerald did not reach that road. Every age has its own predilections; the Victorian age was at times quite void of sex.

It is feasible that if he had led an actual sex life the Rubáiyát might not have been done. Small towns like Woodbridge are not precisely examples of discretion, and not for nothing had FitzGerald called his boat the *Scandal,* for, according to him, scandal was the town's staple industry. If he had had any sort of sexual relations the echo of them would have reverberated even as far as my time—which is another reason I feel justified in believing that, physically, FitzGerald led an entirely sexless life.

It was a very different story where his mind was concerned. There the flames of passion continuously kindled by the heart roared and leaped. All the emotions his body had not had the chance to practice were rampant in his mind; and all his loves were men. It is not for me to say whether his was a happy state of affairs and whether it would not have been better for him to marry (he did marry but not in the true sense) than to burn, but the fact remains that he did burn, and from the distance of the dead yet unburied years one can still feel the glow of that heat.

None of the men he loved so dearly had the slightest homosexual tendencies. Poshy, for instance, would have roared with laughter at the thought of it. On the other hand, Omar Khayyám must have led with Eastern ease a pretty active pederast existence if and when he felt so disposed. And that, one way or the other, proves my point.

It was said that FitzGerald had been in love with two women: Caroline Crabbe and Elisabeth Cowell. There is no evidence of it, albeit he was devoted to both of them. He had many women friends and those friendships thrived, often without personal contact. He saw little of Fanny Kemble after her marriage to Pierce Butler and her departure to America; yet he wrote well-nigh more letters to her than to anybody else.

His mother's personality had surely a lot to do with his attitude to sex; let it, however, not be imagined that he was a soulful, effeminate man. No white lilies for him; his pastimes were mainly robust, and so was his sense of humor. Those who called him effeminate insinuated; men are often called effeminate if they do not conform. His love of bright colors, his passion for nasturtiums, his eccentric mode of dressing influence me not at all in reaching the above conclusion. His life, his work speak in support of it.

Before we embark on his relationship with William Kenworthy Browne, a relationship which at any rate produced *Euphranor* and, far more important, gave FitzGerald some altogether happy hours, his life around the time he met and loved Browne deserves description.

They met in 1831, soon after Thackeray had gone to Germany. They met in a boarding house where both of them stayed. Browne was the son of Joseph Browne of Caldwell House, near Bedford. In the same year FitzGerald had his first train ride.

Between 1831 and 1835 FitzGerald roamed about a lot: Naseby, Wherstead Lodge, a visit to Spedding at Mirehouse, by Bassenthwaite Lake, where they were joined by Alfred Tennyson. Then more travels, more reading, and even more copying of manuscripts in the British Museum. In 1835 came a halt: Boulge Hall.

In those years of rambling, while the friendship with the seven-years-younger Browne grew, FitzGerald had begun to collect pictures. His taste was quite catholic. He could admire a Titian as well as a third-rate water color by Tom Churchyard, the Woodbridge lawyer. He loved, too, the theater, but in later life he could love it only in retrospect. Irving came too late and could not please him. It was no fault of Irving's; he could not be blamed for having been born thirty years after FitzGerald.

Yet FitzGerald was not always a biased critic. His attitude toward two great singers shows the shrewdness and shortcomings of his opinions. The two in question were Braham and Pasta.

"Braham," he said, "was so great in spite of his vulgarity." That indeed was sound criticism, for John Braham, though a great singer, was given to vulgarity in no mean manner. It is recorded of him that once when he sang before the Queen—still the young Victoria without her weeds—he sang the National Anthem. That is meet and proper, but when he reached the line: "On Thee our hopes we fix," he changed it to "On her our hopes we fix." In case he was not completely understood, he raised a finger, indicating the Queen. She blushed. That is a good-enough picture of the first singer, and though FitzGerald's judgments were considered brusque, harsh, and often ill-tempered, at least in the case of Braham he was right.

The second singer in question, Pasta, raised different emotions in him. FitzGerald loved music, understood music, and there was, as the Rubáiyát and the letters show, music in his ear. Yet emotion meant more to him. He admired Pasta, considered her the greatest singer of all time; and indeed she was great, hers was a wonderful voice, she had been the friend of Stendhal, and she was a performer of great merit. But she was no longer so in FitzGerald's day. When FitzGerald heard her, she was already old, and the voice gone. This is what H. F. Chorley said of her around that time:

> Nobody ever sang the great air from Pacini's *Niobe* "*Il suave e bel contento*" as Madame Pasta did—though everyone had tried to sing it. Her execution of it at a provincial concert long ago marks a period in my musical experiences. When she essayed to repeat it at a concert for the Italian cause given some twenty years later—past middle age, out of practice, and with her voice in a state of wretched dilapidation (for which my epithet is not too strong)—not a change, not a cadenza of the old times was left out. She called for them all, though "they would not come."

Yet she was wonderful for FitzGerald, the greatest singer in the world. Even Jenny Lind, the young, the fresh, could not impress him as much. It was his love for the forlorn damsel, his sense of chivalry which made his heart go out to the brave old warrior and the cracked voice. For old times' sake, though he had not known those old times. . . . So accurate about Braham and so emotional about Pasta. . . .

His chivalrous attitude which could influence his judgment, his very love of chivalry and of the forlorn damsel are all proof that however much he turned his back on the pre-Raphaelite movement, its influence was with him because it was of his time. One can be an Unvictorian Victorian, but only up to a point. Alas, our age is always with us, even if we seem unaffected by it. The refined man of letters today who, with his eyes turned to a far more elegant period, dreams of Madame du Deffand, can do so but in triplicate form.

Before I sketch in the background of the times of W. K. Browne, there is one more thing which strikes me about the FitzGerald of Boulge: it is that he had not yet reached the age at which he was born. His young years were still a burden to him. On the other hand, Browne remained young till his death.

As one passes Bredfield Pump Corner, the first field of Boulge Hall estate appears, flat and, in my time, with hedges pretty untidy. The road then forks and there is a signpost saying: To Boulge Hall. The local builder, rather a friend of mine, painted a hand on that signpost and, if the direction the hand indicates is followed, one lands at Debach. A few cottages to the right, and before one reaches the white gate, there is Boulge Cottage to the right. It is not the same cottage in which FitzGerald lived. The original cottage burned down before the First World War, but the new cottage was built more or less on the same lines. Now Lady (Dorothy) White lives there. The estate had belonged to her late husband, Sir Robert Eaton White. After his death she sold the estate to the present owners, Corpus Christi College of Cambridge, and went to live at the Cottage.

After John FitzGerald's death the original Cottage was left deserted. I read somewhere an enthusiastic description of the Cottage by an enthusiastic admirer of FitzGerald. He spoke of the dark empty rooms and then, as it happens with admirers, he conjured up for his readers' benefit FitzGerald in the company of his friends, the self-styled Woodbridge Wits.

The first three years after the family moved to the Hall, FitzGerald lived on and off with them, then he went to the Cottage, to be alone and his own master. He had desired the Cottage ever since he had come to the Hall. He stayed at the Cottage for sixteen years. The Cottage had two rooms. One was his study, the other the bedroom. The walls, he said, were thin as sixpence and damp. But there were the trees. He had a married couple looking after him; the husband was a veteran of Waterloo. The house was crowded with books; there was a bust of Shakespeare but no wardrobe. Anyway, he had very few garments. Three times a week a man came from Woodbridge to shave him. In the mornings he usually sat in slippers and dressing gown.

If he wished to go to the Hall it took him less than five minutes. The walk through the park is a fine walk and the third oak on the right as one goes from Cottage to Hall is one of the best I know. Some of the trees were probably in his days, too, the abode of dark, thief-like jackdaws, birds for which somehow one has little sympathy.

In the winter it was grim at the damp Cottage. There was the frozen road, the snow with the castigating wind that made the trees cry like children. The spring was exquisite with daffodils and cowslips, the leaves young, not yet cabbagy, not yet covered with caterpillars.

FitzGerald had first a large dog, then a Skye terrier, a parrot, and a cat. He smoked, he read, and went for walks. His inner circle of friends was continuously around him. He practiced vegetarianism, though not too passionately, and his years were slowly catching up with him. George Crabbe the Third thus describes his life at the Cottage:

When he was at Boulge Cottage he had a Skye terrier. He had a woman called Mrs. Faiers [wife of the Waterloo man, both buried in Boulge churchyard] he would never ring the bell for her. [It must have astounded the local gentry whenever he opened the door which he mostly did.] E. FG. had a tenor voice accurate but not good. Once in driving with him we saw a beggar & his child sitting at the roadside, tired. He made me stop, he gave the man 1s. He afterwards said to me, That gave me great pleasure!

While E. FG. was at Boulge he always got up early, ate his very small breakfast, stood at his desk reading or writing all the morn, walked with his Skye terrier & then often finished the day by spending the evening with us or the Bartons. He did not visit with the neighbouring gentlefolks as he hated a set dinner party.

Crabbe confessed that when FitzGerald went on his slow walks with the dog, he, still a boy, was rather afraid of him. Everything at the Cottage was most hospitable, but not comfortable.

And now I take at random FitzGerald's own words to illustrate that life which was the background to his friendship with the man at Bedford. To Frederic Tennyson he wrote in 1844:

. . . I tell you that we had the mildest winter known: but as good weather, when it does come in England is always unseasonable, and as an old proverb says that a green Yule makes a fat kirkyard, so it has been with us: the extraordinary fine season has killed heaps of people with influenza, debilitated others for their lives long, worried everybody with colds etc. I have had three influenzas: but that is no wonder: for I live in a hut with walls as thin as sixpence: windows that don't shut: a clay soil safe beneath my feet: a thatch perforated by lascivious sparrows over my head. Here I sit, read, smoke, and become very wise, and am already quite beyond earthly things.

The clay soil of Boulge, it must be admitted, could be pretty embarrassing. When it was hot, the surface broke and you could break your ankle; when it was wet, you sank deep into it. Boulge is the spiritual home of muddy boots.

In despair at the sight of all that wet clay and the dull pollard trees, FitzGerald wished, though not seriously, to live in a pleasant country, for the clay, the trees, and the regular hedges had not even the merit of being bleak on a grand scale. But on he stayed for sixteen years. He traveled from time to time. In 1846 and 1847 he was mostly away, in London to see and buy pictures, listen to music, see Thackeray and Alfred Tennyson, in Norfolk with his sister, Mrs. Kerrich, but chiefly in Bedford with Browne.

I must [he said of an evening when he went to dine with Bernard Barton] soon stir and look about for my greatcoat, brush myself etc. It blows a harrico, as Theodore Hook used to say, and will rain before I get to Woodbridge. Those poor mistaken lilac buds there out of the window! and an old Robbin ruffled up to his thickest, sitting mournfully under them, quite disheartened. For you must know the mild winter is just giving way to a remarkably severe spring. . . .

In the evenings he played the piano, Handel's choruses being his favorites. He played the piano well, and he said he had acquired the true John Bull style of music. Grumbling or not grumbling, he truly loved the Cottage and the dull countryside. When he was in London, staying at 19 Charlotte Street where he used to indulge in much toasting of cheese, he declared that London was hateful to him and all he longed for was to fly into the clear air of the country. The people in the London streets, clever, composed, satirical, selfish, well-dressed, were not a patch in looks, for example, on Mr. Reynolds, then the vicar of Boulge.

In his enthusiasm and longing for the country he tried to persuade even Carlyle to leave his filthy Chelsea, but Jane preferred to stay. A cloud passing overhead is a cloud on its way to Boulge. If he had radishes for breakfast, he nearly had tears in his eyes because with radishes comes the flavor of the earth "that brings all the delicious gardens of the world back into one's soul." When he returned to Boulge, then it was rural vegetation again.

I read [he said in the month of May] of mornings, the same old books over and over again, having no command of new ones: walk with my great black dog of an afternoon, and at evening sit with open windows, up to which China roses climb, with my pipe, while the blackbirds and thrushes begin to rustle bedwards in the garden, and the nightingale to have the neighbourhood to herself. . . . And such verdure! white clouds moving over the new-fledged tops of oak trees, and acres of grass thriving with buttercups. How old to tell of, how new to see!

Little, from nature's aspect, has changed at Boulge since FitzGerald's day. May there has a beauty of its own with the cowslips like a yellow sea with green waves, and the cuckoo is like a not unpleasant conscience.

On late May evenings the nightingales sang at their best. The dusk was on the water lilies in the two small ponds; the surface of the lake began to attend to the oncoming moon and one felt, as FitzGerald had felt, that it was better to have nature than any picture. From the window he would turn to a long-necked bottle on the table with three flowers now just in it: a tuft of rhododendron, a tuft of scarlet geranium, and a tuft of white gillyflower.

A fine May it was with Spedding and Browne staying at the Cottage, one representing the *vita contemplativa*, the other the *vita attiva*. Then to London again in June, moaning for Boulge, the Deben, and even the collier sloop going into the wide world as the sun sank. Then an evening with Carlyle, who was as usual very gloomy about the affairs of the world, which, it must be admitted, would not worry the collier sloop.

Boulge once more, and the summer passed with reading, a little gardening, and then came the autumn with the same faces, the same thoughts occurring at the same turns of road:

This [he said] is all I have to tell of: nothing at all added—but the summer gone. My garden is covered with yellow and brown leaves and a man is digging up the garden beds before my window, and will plant some roots and bulbs for next year. My parsons come and smoke with me, etc. "The round of life from hour to hour" alluding doubtless to a mill-horse.

Winter came. He sat beside the fire, the old woman in the kitchen, the dog and cat on the rug. The only event of the winter was his putting up a trough round the eaves to carry off the wet. It was, he believed, better to be at Boulge with the cold and wet clay than to watch the impudence of the Londoners. A country fog, he thought, stinks only *per se*. The more he went to London the less he liked it, but still he went. The wickedness of London appalled him. He liked, however, to be appalled. He also liked to upbraid himself for his idleness. Idleness he considered a heavy business, and heavily it sat on his shoulders which already had begun to stoop. He was putting on weight—fourteen stones. And he read and copied out and read the same thing again.

Books he read from beginning to end, no forgetting, no skipping. A book for him was not only an intellectual adventure but an adventure, almost, of flesh and blood. He tried not to forget what he had read but, if the memory of his adventure began to dim, he returned to it and the book was read once more. Truly he was not as idle as he pretended, but till very late in life his sense of guilt about his idleness was a constant companion.

When his friend W. F. Pollock was made Master of the Court of Exchequer, in his congratulatory letter FitzGerald spoke more of his own idleness than of Pollock's appointment. However, one does not only nurture one's guilt; now and then one gets on quite well with it. It is food for not altogether unpleasant thought and it is a hotbed of excuses. "I," he triumphantly said, "pretend to no Genius but to Taste: which according to my aphorism is the feminine of Genius."

In winter it snowed heavily.

Snow over the ground [he said]. We have our wonders of inundation in Suffolk also, I can tell you. For three weeks ago such floods came, that an old woman was carried off as she was retiring from a beer house at 9 p.m. and drowned. She was probably half seas over before she left the beer house.

And three nights ago I looked out about ten o'clock at night, before going to bed. It seemed perfectly still; frosty and the stars shining bright. I heard a continuous moaning sound, which I knew to be, not that of an infant exposed, or female ravished, but of the sea more than ten miles off! What little wind there was carried to us the murmurs of the waves circulating round these coasts so far over flat country. But people here think that this sound so heard is not from the waves that break, but a kind of prophetic voice from the body of the sea itself announcing great gales. Sure enough we have got them, however heralded. Now I say that all this shows that we in this Suffolk are not so completely given over to prose and turnips as some would have us. I always said that being near the sea, and being able to catch a glimpse of it from the tops of the hills, and of houses, redeemed Suffolk from dullness; and at all events that our turnip fields, dull in themselves, were at least set all round with an undeniably poetic element.

The above I quoted from the postscript of a letter he wrote to Frederic Tennyson. For idleness he may well have apologized up to a point, but of dullness he needed to have no fear. He could be bored and lonely, but dullness was not his. Suffolk or no Suffolk, no landscape can be dull if observed with interested eyes.

His background was not only the Cottage and the wind and flowers but his friends, too. In a sense, first among them was Alfred Smith, the son of Job Smith who was the agent at Boulge and farmed the Hall Farm, that is to say, the home farm. Many evenings he spent with the Smiths, and usually the handsome Vicar of Debach and Boulge (now Boulge belongs to the parish of Bredfield) was there, too. But his true affection was for Alfred. He gave him plenty of presents, including once a half-crown for the boy to buy himself a cheap toy. In those days, when half-crowns still stretched a long way, one could buy toys and toys with such a coin; but of such practical matters Fitz-Gerald knew little and cared less. Alfred Smith later on became his first reader.

That reader business is somewhat curious. From time to time FitzGerald believed that his eyesight troubled him, and then he would engage someone to read for him. After a while he would decide that his eyes were much better and dispense with the reader. Long stretches of doing without a reader would follow, then suddenly the need for a reader would come over him again. It seems that the whole thing was just one of Old Fitz's crotchets (I am not speaking of his old age when his eyes, as it happens to most old men, were becoming weak).

When he read to himself, his reading was mostly the Classics and his own studies, but his readers read accounts of murders, trials, and, in his old days, every stage of the Tichborne case. If not a crotchet, then it was a form of relaxation. He could soon become bored by the reader and dismiss him brusquely. Beside readers and their reading, he had scrapbooks which he called his Common Place Books. I saw some of them at Trinity Library; they were an amazing collection. Here are some of the headings to his notes:

President Henault's Memoirs
The Shepperd's Grove
Horne's Collection of Discourses
Lines in the Pocket Book of Mr. Whites—a dissenting Minister of Yarmouth, reputed mad, who killed himself
Weather Cocks on Churches
Lord Chatham
Binning's Persia

He had a collection of press cuttings which contained accounts of murders, anecdotes, and Napoleon's only letter in English; also notes on restoration of paintings.

For Alfred Smith to be FitzGerald's reader was more an entertainment than work: presents, ample tea; but Alfred disliked Mrs. Faiers because she strongly smelt of snuff. FitzGerald was devoted to Alfred, took him now and then to London, and here once more one feels that in friendship FitzGerald never took the middle course. Alfred, at any rate, remained his staunch friend all his life and when FitzGerald, because of brother John's proximity, left the Cottage (meanwhile the Smiths had moved to Farlingay Hall), he went to live with the Smiths. It must have needed plenty of patience and affection to look after such a lodger.

FitzGerald liked to be surrounded by farmers, seamen, and fishermen. When he came down from Cambridge he chose indolence and literature instinctively and with no hesitation as his life companions, instead of choosing—as he might have done—indolence and hunting, shooting, and fishing. Yet he loved all men who pursued an outdoor existence. The farmers, the seamen, the fishermen were as much to his liking as Tennyson, Spedding, and Carlyle. He had dignity but no condescension, and thus the country folk were his respectful, jolly friends.

Once Alfred Smith gave a Christmas party at Farlingay Hall. FitzGerald, who would have refused an invitation to any of the local squires' parties, was present.

My friend [he related afterwards] Alfred Smith (Farmer) gave a Xmas Party & a Xmas Tree: all the Company delighted when suddenly his Father-in-law, a ponderous Man, silenced the Company for awhile by proposing an Enigma.

"Why is Alfred's Xmas Tree like the Ipswich Agricultural Show?" Nobody could guess, but after keeping all in Suspense for some while, the Author of this Enigma was delivered of the Solution also—

"Because it's a great Success."

Next to the Smiths he frequently saw Bernard Barton (with whom, unsympathetically, I will deal later), Churchyard, the solicitor-painter, and the Reverend George Crabbe the Second. This circle dubbed itself the Woodbridge Wits. W. B. Donne used to visit with him and so did Groome.

George Crabbe had by then published the life of his father. He was a kind, friendly man and the one member of the Woodbridge Wits to whom FitzGerald's fine income mattered little. He was given to enthusiasm of an endearing kind. When the Great Exhibition came onto the world, he hurried to London to inspect it. On his return Groome asked him what he thought of it.

"Thought of it my dear sir!" cried Crabbe. "When I entered that vast emporium of the world's commerce, I lifted my arms and shouted for amazement."

It is, therefore, easy to understand that he and FitzGerald were good friends.

What, one cannot help asking oneself, was FitzGerald like in company, and as one asks that question one pictures him, not quite involuntarily, entering to-day a London cocktail party of the more literate kind. He would not be a success. He would talk to the few people he liked; in fact, not only talk to them but take possession of them. With them he would laugh but he would watch them jealously and, if they wished to speak to someone else, he would be hurt and unhappy.

For the rest of the party he would have no words, no time. If a stranger, out of sheer politeness, spoke to him, FitzGerald might easily turn his back on him. The general verdict would be that here was a sullen, ill-mannered man, badly dressed, hands not too clean, and, as it is said, with nothing to offer; but the few who knew him would feel at that party better men because Old Fitz was there. And this was the same Old Fitz who, after Thackeray had broken his heart (Thackeray would have been the toast of the cocktail party), turned to William Kenworthy Browne, who was of the world in which success at a party mattered a lot.

Fitzgerald at times was a sound judge of character and, as it often happens with such judges, he heeded not his judgment. When he met Browne he summed him up correctly and with shrewd eyes.

He had shot at rooks and rabbits & trained horses & dogs and I—have looked at him: and well I may while I can for his like is not to be seen. Perhaps also he will not be long to be looked at: for there are signs of decay about him: and his very perfection of nature somehow forbodes a short continuance: and as dramatists are said to prematurely kill such characters as they find difficult to sustain, so it is that Nature cannot or will not carry on her finest creations through the five acts. Indeed there is something anomalous and perhaps insupportable in the appearance of one perfect character in a world of imperfection & inconsistency.

You do not know this fellow & I shall probably see less of him year by year—But I have said what I have said & as the Doctor says, perhaps I am the better for having said it.

For a man given to *Schwärmerei* it is surprisingly clearsighted to sum up thus the man to whom the *Schwärmerei* so fully went out. Nature did in fact give Browne looks, health, buoyancy, a gift for happiness, a happy married life, and then it gave him an unnecessarily tragic death. But while he lived, he gave Fitz-Gerald happiness. He was a creature full of sun, without qualms, and everything sat, provided it did sit, lightly on his shoulders.

FitzGerald did not ask for much: his presence, when it was convenient for Browne, and happy thoughts about him when Browne was not present. He lent Browne money, but to lend was not only a sign of his generosity: loans were one more tie with his friends, one more reason for the friend to be unable to get out of his life. Their friendship was by no means plain sailing. FitzGerald could be, and often was, jealous and acrimonious. Browne was a man of no intellectual inclinations, and FitzGerald would find an outlet for his temper and jealousy by nastily squashing Browne's quite innocent remarks. There followed repentance and with tears in his eyes he would say, "I hate myself for them."

And always with him was the thought that one day their friendship would have to end, and the fact that Carlyle had said that no one is expected to be happy was meagre consolation.

Browne was a charming, average person. Thackeray referred to him as Little Browne, which was not to FitzGerald's taste, for he was convinced that Browne had a rare intuition into Men, Matters, and even Matters of Art. Browne was fond of shooting, hunting, and fishing. FitzGerald, for his sake, did a little fishing, but for the other two sports he had no liking. Because Browne was good at them and because he himself was either not interested in them or could not excel at them, FitzGerald's admiration was unbounded. FitzGerald asked for and received high intellectual pleasures from Donne, Thackeray, the Tennysons, Spedding, Allen, Carlyle, and Groome, all men of gifts and culture; in Browne, and later far more in Posh, those gifts were conspicuously absent. Those two friendships were in a sense mental escapism, but such escapes are seldom wholehearted, as FitzGerald was to discover on the evening when he took Posh to see *The Merchant of Venice* and Posh slept through it.

And so it often was with Browne. FitzGerald would be annoyed at Browne's lack of learning and intellectual achievements, and his angry outbursts and harsh rebukes were, naturally, the results of his unjustified annoyance. But there they were: the handsome, dapper Browne in perfectly polished hunting boots, auburn locks; and the large, stooping FitzGerald, badly dressed, his hair going. To understand FitzGerald's devotion is not difficult, notwithstanding the great mental difference between them, but one is surprised that a gay, average country gentleman, keen on gun and horse, should have had affection for an, at times, not too pleasant, eccentric bear. Yet it is indisputable that Browne was fond of FitzGerald, was a good friend to him, and had to put up with a lot. What was admirable and even awe-inspiring in FitzGerald's mind was past Browne's understanding; therefore it is a moving thought that all that Browne, with his limitations, could like were the kindness, the humor, and the great heart; and that, to Browne's glory, did for him suffice.

The time they spent together—and around 1840 FitzGerald spent as much time as he could put in with Browne—was spent mostly on Browne's own ground, in Bedfordshire. Their pastime was fishing, FitzGerald fishing because Browne was fond of it.

"For in half an hour," FitzGerald joyously declared, "I shall seek my Piscator and we shall go to a Village two miles off and fish and have tea in a pot-house and so walk home. For all which idle ease I think I must be damned."

He was not yet to be damned. From Bedfordshire he would take Browne to Boulge, so that they might be longer together. Again, time is handed over to Browne—though not completely, for when they went to a lodging house at Lowestoft, after Browne had taught a big black dog to retrieve and they had played with the neighbor's children, after shooting gulls and going out in boats, FitzGerald instructed Browne in the first five propositions of Euclid. Browne, he told Allen, had certainly made him happier than any man living. "Sometimes," he admitted, "I behave very ill to him and am much ashamed of myself; but enough of this."

During my time at Boulge I often motored through Lowestoft and, whenever I was there or went through it, somehow it always rained. Consequently in my mind Lowestoft is more associated with the harsh, beer-sodden figure of Posh than of the gentle Browne with auburn locks. Browne was one of those rare beings who have a sunshine of their own. FitzGerald had not; and it is good to know that about a hundred years ago there was a man who with his innocent warmth made FitzGerald truly happy.

This is becoming an admission on my part. When I

settled down at Boulge my first week-end guest came. It was my friend Roger Senhouse, and it was he who suggested that around me lay not only the material but the atmosphere, too, of a study on FitzGerald. At the moment, I felt no special enthusiasm. In the library I had almost the entire "English Men of Letters" series. I took down A. C. Benson's *Edward FitzGerald*. The first lines were not inspiring. "The life," said Benson, "that is here proposed to depict was a life singularly devoid of incident." I felt like leaving the whole thing at that. But in a curious, undefinable manner, the trees of Boulge, the chimes of Old Nelly, the daffodils, the cowslips, the nightingales, and the Deben all began to spin their charm around me and that charm was of FitzGerald; and thus it happens that two years later, the two years having been spent practically with FitzGerald, I feel gratitude to Browne for having given him happiness.

In his own manner FitzGerald gave, too. Browne was fond of target shooting, so FitzGerald would go out pistol shooting, too, and, naturally, miss at ten yards. Still, it made him happy. And he who loved Titian, and could haughtily criticize Constable, bought Browne two pictures: one was of a Crome cottage and the other a hawking picture. Browne was delighted with them and because of his delight FitzGerald threw to the winds his own taste in paintings.

138

In 1844 Browne decided to marry. FitzGerald was against it and tried to dissuade him. Later, when Fitz-Gerald was going to be married, it was Browne's turn to speak against it, the difference being that whereas Browne's marriage turned out to be a happy one, Fitz-Gerald's was hardly a marriage, notwithstanding the misery and unhappiness it caused him.

He went to Browne's wedding. In those days Browne was still clean-shaven; after his marriage he wore a mustache and whiskers. He was twenty-six at the time.

"Browne," mourned FitzGerald, "is married and I shall see but little of him for the future. I have laid by my rod and line by the willows of the Ouse for ever."

To Barton he wrote, "This time ten years I first went to ride and fish with him about the river Ouse—he was then 18—quick to love and quick to fight—full of confidence, generosity and the glorious spirit of Youth."

Nevertheless, he became as great friends with Mrs. Browne as Johnson had been incapable of becoming with Mrs. Boswell. He stayed with them on and off till Browne's death, and his liking for Mrs. Browne survived the husband. The Brownes after their marriage went to live at Goldington Hall, two miles from Bedford.

As I have said before, his adulation of Browne was balanced by a certain shrewd judgment; Browne's faults and mistakes were not glossed over by FitzGerald. In

1848 Browne, after a visit to Bedfordshire by the Sage, looked after a horse that belonged to Carlyle. He made out his bill which was sent to Carlyle by FitzGerald.

I find that I did not enclose W. Browne's very off hand Bill; here it is.

Copy of Bill

Expense of keeping the horse	£6
Bringing to London	1.10
Horse being attended for the accident	1.10

Admittedly it was rather offhand.

Browne for the rest of his life lived a full country existence: wife, children, horses, gun, sitting on the Magistrates' Bench, even some soldiering with the Bedfordshire Regiment of Regular Militia. During the war of 1854 he was a captain and on garrison duty in Galway. That separation irked FitzGerald; and the final separation came in 1859. On June 20 of that year he wrote to Carlyle:

Geldestone Hall, Beccles
June 20/59

Dear Carlyle, Very soon after I called and saw Mrs. Carlyle I got a violent Cold, which (being neglected) flew to my Ears, and settled into such a Deafness I couldn't hear the Postman knock nor the Omnibus roll. When I began (after more than a Month) to begin recovering of this (though still so deaf as to determine not to be a Bore to any one else) I heard from Bedford that my poor W. Browne (who got you a Horse some fifteen years ago) had been fallen on and crushed all through the middle Body by one of his own: and I then kept expecting every Postman's knock was to announce his Death. He kept on however in a shattered Condition which the Doctors told me scarce any one else would have borne a Week; kept on for near two Months, and then gave up his honest Ghost. I went to bid him Farewell: and then came here (an Address you remember) only going to Lowestoft (on the Sea) to entertain my old George Crabbe's two Daughters, who, now living inland, are glad of a sight of the old German Sea, and also perhaps of poor Me . . .

Browne had been out hunting and, riding home in the dusk, he raised his whip and struck a hound that was lagging behind. The lash touched his horse's head, the horse reared and fell back, crushing Browne. He was taken home, almost broken in half. Patiently, bravely he remained wretched and alive for nine weeks. Fitz-Gerald came to the dying man. He was at first not allowed to see his friend, but one morning, after he had made the resolution to show no unhappiness nor tears, he was taken into Browne's room. It was no longer the gay lad he had known, but a face like that of Charles I just after decapitation, and the poor shattered body hidden underneath the blanket. For eight weeks that poor body had lain like that; such a case the doctor said he had never known before. But there was one great consolation, for Browne spoke to him.

"Old fellow—Fitz," he said, and then, in spite of

141

his resolution, FitzGerald broke down. It took Browne's body nine weeks to die.

Around the time my thoughts reached Browne's death, the Omar Khayyám Club came down to Fitz-Gerald's grave. If you leave the drive to go to the churchyard, you have before you an iron gate, which opens with difficulty. The road that leads to the grave is in poor condition. The trees are high and the rooks deafening. Each spring the Pest Officer wrote to me, asking what I intended to do with the rooks. I replied I would myself attend to them, which meant I would shoot them. In 1946 I shot over three hundred rooks.

There being plenty of undergrowth, it was not easy to find the rooks after they had flopped to the ground. So I took with me the son of the cowman, Andrew by name, aged nine and bloodthirsty. He was an ambitious boy: he wanted to become like Joe Louis, not in color but in boxing prowess. He assured me he would, when the time came, bash in everybody's head. His momentary desire, however, was to put a bird of sorts into a cage he had acquired. If a rook was not yet completely dead, he wanted to take it home and put it in the cage.

"Don't be silly," I said. "Besides, it's cruel."

"That one," he said later when another dying rook was picked up, "it's not dead. I'll take it home and put it into the cage."

142

I did not let him.

Eventually he disillusioned me. The following autumn I asked him to come and beat for me on a Saturday when we were going to shoot pheasants. He said he would not come because he was going to the cinema. I tried to argue with him, but it was in vain. One more country lad lost.

So, past the rickety gate and the noisy rooks, came the Omar Khayyám Club, led by Lord Horder and Mr. James Laver. Toward the Omar Khayyám Club I felt and still feel guilty. The reason is simple enough. At the head of FitzGerald's grave there is a rose, or rather something that had been a rose. Before the rose is a plate with this inscription:

"This Rose-Tree raised in Kew Gardens from seed brought by William Simpson, artist traveller, from the grave of Omar Khayyám at Naish á púr, was planted by a few admirers of Edward FitzGerald in the name of the Omar Khayyám Club."

There was, alas, no rose on Omar Khayyám's grave. One can easily picture the artist-traveler arriving at Nishapur, brimming with devotion to Omar and the Rose. The rose he wanted and some courteous native, with the politeness and the eye for baksheesh of the Oriental, promptly obliged. It would be interesting to know whence, after all, the rose came. Still, intention is what matters.

A few months before the descent on Boulge, I had been a guest at the yearly dinner of the Omar Khayyám Club and, when answering for the guests, I was tactless enough to tell the truth about the rose. The Club, I must admit, took it without flinching.

After they had viewed the rose, they came round to the house for a drink, and Mr. Victor Bridges, a Club member, told me that as far as he could remember there were somewhere or other about twenty letters FitzGerald had written to Mrs. Browne after his friend's death. It was all vague in his memory, but he suggested that I should write to the *Times Literary Supplement* and that might bring results. I wrote and, as it happens on such occasions, a spate of extraordinary letters came my way. It has always been, and will remain for me, a matter of surprise how people find time to write to one on subjects they know nothing about and about which they care even less.

One letter did amuse me. I was informed by the writer that she had known Edward FitzGerald when he was a mining engineer in South America. I see no reason why there should not have been a mining engineer in South America called Edward FitzGerald, and probably his life was more eventful than FitzGerald's. Nevertheless, it seemed to me that a reader of the *Times Literary Supplement* should have hesitated before taking for granted that my Edward FitzGerald could be no one other than the mining engineer she knew.

Then there was, needless to say, the letter from the insurance company which would help me to buy a house; a copy of my own letter to the *Supplement*, sent by a press-cutting agency which wanted a subscription; and then came a letter from Browne's grandson, telling me that the letters were in his possession, but that he would not show them to me because they dealt only with private matters.

It was not for me to argue with him. After nearly a hundred years, letters lose their strictly private value, and among those letters there might have been one or two which would have delighted FitzGerald's admirers or might have thrown a tiny ray of light on one or other aspect of FitzGerald's turn of mind or thoughts. With the brusque refusal I imagined the matter was closed.

A few days later came a letter in a fine, precise handwriting, the sort of handwriting which, what with typewriters and the telephone, has almost joined the dodo. It was from a Mr. C. Charles Paine, who had a few FitzGerald letters, and if I wished to see them he would be glad to show them to me. Among the letters was one written to Mrs. Browne. I fixed an appointment with him, and my wife and I drove to London.

My car at the time, an Armstrong-Siddeley sports saloon, will remain for me not only an accessory but also part and parcel of Boulge. Because Boulge was four miles from the nearest bus stop, that car became the gondola of East Suffolk, the bridge between myself and the world. I had bought that car from my friend Mr. Cyril Connolly and once, when an enthusiastic American publisher came to stay with me and I had picked him up at Ipswich station, he joyfully exclaimed: "You live in FitzGerald's house and drive in Connolly's car. What more do you want!" Alas, human nature is never truly satisfied.

So, in that car we drove to London and went to the Boltons, where Mr. Paine lived. It was September, the leaves still undying, the dust still the dust the summer had left behind. It was quiet in the Boltons and I thought of Mr. Paine's handwriting. His house, too, was like his handwriting: elegant, quiet, and of a world now hopelessly gone. Mr. Paine was short, slim, well over eighty, with fine teeth and a low voice. He showed us three letters which he had bought at a Red Cross sale during the war.

"FitzGerald," he said, "had always been my hero."

We worked out how old Mr. Paine had been when FitzGerald died. It turned out that FitzGerald had been not only his hero but the hero of his youth.

I asked him if I could buy the letters. Mr. Paine gently

said the letters were not for sale. In a year or two, he added, those letters probably would be for sale, though he would know nothing about it. On the other hand, I could make whatever use I wanted of the letters. I suggested that my wife should copy them. During our stay in Cambridge, as I have mentioned in the preface, she had mastered FitzGerald's handwriting, not an easy task, for he wrote a very poor hand. He could if he wanted write legibly, but apparently he did not often want to. Mr. Paine said no, he would copy out the letters himself and send me the copies. It would have been ill-mannered to insist. He asked us to stay for tea, but I had an appointment for which I was already late, so we said we were sorry but had to go. When we took our leave I told him I would send him a copy of the book when it appeared. He said in that case I had better hurry up with it.

A week later I received the following letter with the copies of the letters:

Herewith the copies of the FitzGerald letters. I have left conjecture matter in pencil. E.F. ought to have written better as he was not an old man according to our modern notions. The year of the Woolner letter is fixed by the postmark.

I am afraid I was rather inhospitable but you did not jump at my offer of tea. I am sorry.

I wish success to your book and am

Yours very truly,

C. Charles Paine.

The Woolner letter will be quoted when I reach Posh. The letter written to Mrs. Browne was sent off from Woodbridge on December 30, 1871. Thus more than twenty years after Browne's death his wife, that is to say the woman Browne had married, was still in Fitz-Gerald's thoughts.

I won't let this year die without a word of Remembrance of Old Days, & wishes of good for those that are coming.

I hope that the Mortgage leaves no bitter taste in your mind: I do not think it should do so. Yet it is not to be wondered at if it should. I should like to hear whether you retain Goldington still, if you do not think me unworthy to ask such a question. I have even less events to tell of myself. For, my eyes being in very indifferent order all this year, I have been much less away from home even than before; for I have not been able to read, which was nearly all I had to do in a seaside Lodging: whereas, here, at home, I can dawdle about my Garden, play with the Cat, & look at the Builders adding two new rooms to the home which I built but which I never inhabit. My nieces come there sometimes, as you may know: and I lend it to others now & then, very well pleased to have it made use of. But I ought to make one little excursion before 1872 is out. To no other place than—Naseby—where Carlyle still wants me to put up a Memorial Stone over the Dead whom I exhumed for him 30 years ago. I was quite ready to supply the Stone & the Cost of Labour in fashioning it: but the journey! And to a Place that is nothing but Melancholy to me now! —Yet I believe I *ought* to do this for a Man so justly distinguished as Carlyle, and this, in his later days, the last request that he will probably make to me.

A Boy comes to read to me of a night & we have gone through *all* Tichborne since the case re-opened in November. I have got to be extremely interested in it, but do not know what to think: except that the Claimant will hardly prove his Case so beyond Doubt as to dispossess the present Possessors.

Pray remember me (if you still think me worth it) to your Family: let me hear about yourself & them: & believe me

In spite of Mortgages & all
Yours sincerely
Edward FitzGerald

What became of the mortgage I do not know. Perhaps the letters which I was not allowed to see could have thrown light on it. If the mortgagee was FitzGerald, then Mrs. Browne had surely nothing to worry about. In matters of money FitzGerald was as generous as with his friendships. He went out of his way to help and to lend, for loans and help bound the friend even more to him. Once having lent money which was to be repaid in installments, after a few installments were paid, he declared that sufficed and canceled the debt.

So, long after his death Browne was still with him; and it was for Browne and, as it were, about Browne that he wrote *Euphranor*.

Euphranor is a curious work, mostly a conversation piece. It has not the felicitous balance of style which makes, for example, his *Memorial of Bernard Barton* such pleasure to read. It is believed that he wrote *Euphranor* as a protest against too much learning and too little sport at Cambridge in his time, and that the figure of Phidippus, who was Browne himself, was intended as an example at which undergraduates should aim. If such was the case, then *Euphranor* curiously misfired. To me it seems that it was generated by FitzGerald's desire to explain away the difference in learning between Browne and himself, and it was intended as an apology for his friendship and a vindication of Browne, a vindication in front of FitzGerald himself.

Instead of taking his friends as they were, especially as he had chosen them as such, he either wanted them to rise in qualities above him, or he tried to reason out why they were not like him. He could not reconcile himself with Thackeray's worldliness, Browne's lack of bookishness, nor with Posh's beer.

Euphranor was privately published by John Parker in 1855. It opens in a room in Cambridge. The room is the Doctor's room and FitzGerald is the Doctor. The Doctor is suppose to be practicing in Cambridge, but it is immediately pointed out that he "was pretending to practice." So, even as a fictitious doctor, FitzGerald could not believe that he could work seriously. An undergraduate, Euphranor, arrives. It is Euphranor who ousts Phidippus from the title page, for Phidippus should have been the title. But Euphranor, who is rather a shadow, does, next to the Doctor, most of the talking. Unkindly, one could suggest that though originally Phidippus was intended to be the central figure, FitzGerald had sorrowfully to acknowledge while writing the book that Browne could not be a central figure where erudite talk was concerned.

Another undergraduate arrives, Lexilogus, a true scholar, and the idea is to go by boat to Chesterton. "It was such a day—sun shining—breeze blowing—hedges and leaves in full leaf." Off they go, the three of them, and begin to discuss Chivalry, apparently because Euphranor has accidentally with him Kenelm Digby's *Godefridus* (the first part of *The Broad Stones of Honour*). The Doctor believes that the soul must have a beautiful abode, namely that one should have a fine physique. Since *Euphranor* is written in Plato's manner, it is not surprising that Socrates is then mentioned by Euphranor. One feels what is in the Doctor's mind when he speaks.

"Socrates?" said I. "No; but did not he profess that his Soul was naturally an ugly soul to begin with? Socrates, by the time he had beautified her within, it was too late to re-front her Outside, which had case-hardened, I suppose. But did not he accompany Alcibiades, not only because of his Spiritual, but also of his Physical Beauty, in which, as in the Phidian statues, the Divine Original of Man was supposed to reflect Himself, and which has been accepted as such by Christian Art, and indeed by all Peoples who are furthest removed that of the Beast?"

Socrates-FitzGerald and Alcibiades-Browne would indeed be a fine sight if seen walking beside the Ouse.

The Doctor, Euphranor, and Lexilogus are then joined by Lycion, fashionable and a keen billiard player, and it is quite obscure to me why FitzGerald had to bring him in. He spends most of his time playing billiards in the background. They arrive at the Three Tuns Inn. Euphranor puts set questions which the Doctor answers in detail. The Doctor's talk should give Etonians pleasure for he praises Eton in no mean manner. His praises are high for Winchester, too. Euphranor, who had been to school at Westminster, said in its defense that Eton's own river flows beside it in ampler proportions.

"Though not so sweet," the Doctor replies.

The Doctor cares most for chivalry and knights. And it is, as FitzGerald admitted, Browne of whom the Doctor thinks when "having gotten the bit between my teeth," he maintains

against all Comers that, independent of any bodily action on their part, these, and the like Accomplishments, as you call them, and, I will say, with the Soul incorporate, the habitual Instinct of Courage, Resolution, and Decision, which, together with the Good Humour which good animal Condition goes so far to ensure, do, I say, prepare and arm the Man not only against the greater, but against those minor Trials of Life which are so far harder to encounter because of perpetually cropping up; and thus do cause him to radiate, if through a narrow circle, yet, through that, imperceptibly to the whole world, a happier atmosphere about him than could be inspired by Closet-loads of Poetry, Metaphysics and Divinity.

The heaviness of style is almost embarrassing, quite unworthy of the fine letter writer; but on the other hand it is a loyal defense of Browne. The Doctor and his companions continue on their course and it is nature which is contemplated for the next little while. There were the fields "crop-thick with Daisy, Clover and Buttercup." Then Euphranor quotes from Chaucer, Euphranor certainly having Browne in mind, too.

> *Embrouded was he as it were a Mede,*
> *Alle ful of fresshe Floures, white and rede;*
> *Singing he was, or floyting alle the day;*
> *He was as fresshe as is the moneth of May:*

Discussion on Chaucer follows; afterwards they speak of Shakespeare and Sir Walter Scott (for whom Fitz-Gerald had the deepest admiration); then come Carlyle, Wordsworth, and Burns. All this only leads up to the meeting with Phidippus. Phidippus, as one would expect him to do, arrives on horseback:

"I recognized Phidippus for one of the riders, with two others whom I did not know. I held out my hand,

and call'd out to him as he was passing; and Phidippus drawing up his horse all snorting and agitated with her arrested course, wheel'd back and came alongside with us."

The Doctor persuades him to leave his companions and to join them. The mare Phidippus rides is called Miss Middleton, and she is not happy at being detached from the other horses and relegated to the company of pedestrians—further proof of the magnitude of the Doctor's success in persuading Phidippus to stay with them.

They go to the inn, a meal is ordered. Miss Middleton, a gift from Phidippus's Yorkshireman father, is for the moment the topic of conversation and the Doctor sings a comic song in her honor.

> I'll sing you a Song, and a merry merry Song,
> Concerning our Yorkshire Jen;
> Who never ran with Horse or Mare,
> That ever she cared for a pin.

There is quite a lot more in that vein. It appears that Phidippus does not like sporting ladies. They go to the bowling green, and here Phidippus about rivals the Doctor. It is now time for him to leave them. There will be a boat race in the afternoon and he must see his friends start. And then the amazing thing happens, not to Euphranor or Lexilogus but to Edward FitzGerald, for, after having defended his friend Browne, praised him for his physical qualities in contrast to other people's overgrown brains, he loses his temper with his creation Phidippus, just as in real life he so often did with Browne.

"But Phidippus," so the passage goes, "was engaged to sup with his crew."

"Where you will all be drunk," said I. [The I being the Doctor.]

"No; there," said he, "you are quite mistaken, Doctor."

"Well, well," I said, "away, then, to your race and your supper."

"Μετὰ σώφρονος ἡλικιώτου," added Euphranor smiling.

"A temperate—something or other—"

"Μετὰ, 'with' or 'after,' " said Phidippus putting on his gloves.

"Well, go on, Sir," said I, "Σώφρονος?"

"A temperate—something or other—"

"Ἡλικιώτου?"

"Supper?" he hesitated, smiling— "After a temperate supper?"

"Go down, Sir; go down this instant!" I roar'd out to him as he ran from the bowling-green. And in a few minutes we heard his mare's feet shuffling over the stable threshold, and directly afterwards breaking into a retreating canter beyond.

So there it was. Poor Browne had mixed up the meaning of "companion" with "supper" because his Greek was not good, and FitzGerald's anger was boundless. For the rest of *Euphranor*, which is now soon to end, he does not repent of his anger. Though in life, after such outbursts, he hated himself, in the book he does not. In fact Phidippus is mentioned only twice more. Once shouting on horseback to his crew, "conspicuous over all," and again when he engages himself "in eager conversation with his defeated brethren." Apparently Phidippus has to be humiliated a trifle more, and Doctor FitzGerald takes Euphranor and Lexilogus "under either arm [Lycion having got into better company elsewhere] and walk'd home with them across the meadow leading to the town, whither the dusky troops of Gownsmen with all their confused voices seem'd as it were evaporating in the twilight, while a Nightingale began to be heard among the flowering Chestnuts of Jesus."

This, the last sentence of *Euphranor*, is always quoted by the defenders of the book, trying to create the impression that the whole was written as well. That, however, is not the case. The style is heavy and far too diffuse.

Why FitzGerald imagined that *Euphranor* would or could do anything in favor of less learning and more sport is a mystery. Yet he believed that, or at least pretended to. Today all this is beside the point: it is doubtful if many people will ever read *Euphranor* again (few had at the time), and its intrinsic interest is the sharp light it throws on FitzGerald's friendship with Browne.

Browne's share of the burden of friendship was not always easy to bear, as the incident in *Euphranor* shows. It is a difficult thing to be beloved by one who prefers to love one for qualities which are perhaps not precisely there. Browne's looks, his integrity, his gentleness were easy to love and should have sufficed; but in his pride and jealousy FitzGerald wanted from his friend, too, all he himself could offer. The Doctor's knowledge and range are remarkable. It does not, on the other hand, occur to the Doctor that he, with his knowledge of Greek, might not make so splendid a figure on horseback as Phidippus.

The long and the short of it is that his friendship with Browne was probably the happiest he had, for Browne was good and tolerant of him. And it is curious to contemplate that, given their minds and characteristics, it was more difficult for the handsome squire to love the learned bear than the other way round.

When Browne lay dying, the thought might have come to FitzGerald that if his friend had known more Greek and less about horses he might not then be dying. Nevertheless, his dead friend remained to him "as fresshe as is the moneth of May."

Part Four

MARRIAGE

I F YOU wish to enter the FitzGerald country through Ipswich, then a disappointment is in store for you. It is in many ways a hideous town. True, there is the Orwell, but there are also the main streets, the spreading lifeless suburbs, and many factory chimneys. There is, too, Thoro'fare, and if you go by car you will find out that London traffic jams are child's play in comparison. But Ipswich has its antiquities; the trolley buses look as though they had been designed long before electricity was thought of. So, if one travels by train, it is best to alight at Woodbridge, and if by car, the Ipswich By Pass shows enough of the town well-nigh to disregard the speed limit.

Woodbridge is a graceful town with fine Georgian houses built mostly during the Napoleonic wars. The Artillery was at the time stationed at Woodbridge, and houses had to be built for the officers—hence the Georgian buildings. I, who had motored all over Suffolk and Norfolk, often reflected that, whereas the army which was there to repel the Emperor left behind those fine houses, the army which was to push back the Fuehrer left behind Nissen huts, barbed wire, crumbling anti-tank blocks, and the rest of the hideous paraphernalia of modern war.

Woodbridge is a town of several churches and of the Salvation Army, too. On Sundays, when we went to the Catholic church of Saint Thomas of Canterbury to the ten:thirty Mass, the Salvation Army band was already rallying. The sermon of Father Thomson, our parish priest, began around eleven. This was the hour the band chose to march past the church, in an effort to drown the priest's voice. On Sunday evenings the band used to play in Market Hill between the Shire House and the Bull, quite near to FitzGerald's lodgings.

Woodbridge is a town which is in no hurry, and therefore in many ways it is still the same town Fitz-Gerald knew. At any rate the same interest is still taken in one's neighbor as in the days when FitzGerald named his ship the *Scandal*.

There is still leisure left, and one fine morning, driving into Woodbridge with the sun over the town and the Deben, I gave a lift to a town counselor who lived not far from Farlingay Hall (Woodbridge is in a sense the FitzGerald Museum, and a number of streets, one could say, were left exactly as he saw them last). The counselor said Woodbridge was asleep and what the town needed was factories. I tried to make him understand that the charm of Woodbridge was its half-closed eyes. It was useless to argue with him since he belonged to our day, whereas I like half to close my eyes. Therefore he will probably triumph, and with wide-open eyes some day Woodbridge will glare at its factory chimneys.

If you want, you can turn off the By Pass at the corner where Farlingay Hall stands. After a few minutes' drive you pass FitzGerald's lodgings in Market Hill. If you go down Church Street and turn to the left, you are in Thoro'fare, the main street of the town. It is narrow; complaints about the dense traffic were recorded even a hundred years ago. There is usually a long queue of stationary cars and buses ahead of one, also plenty of hooting, but all good-humored, for nobody is in a hurry. The policeman saunters down, a car backs here onto the pavement, another goes onto the pavement over there, almost but not quite entering a shop, and then, after a nice slice of time, traffic starts again. You drive with many similar halts as far as Melton Hill. Turn to the left and soon you find yourself at Little Grange where FitzGerald lived his last years and died. If you started originally from Boulge Hall, you passed the Cottage and Bredfield House, thus practically spanning his life.

But let it not be thought that Woodbridge is too proud of FitzGerald. At the time when I was trying to collect as many details as I could from people who remembered him, and from others whose parents might have known him, I ran into a wall of indifference. "Well," said one of them, "he lived, he died, and we have other things to think about."

The reason is that he was not popular. Notwithstanding his friends and friendships, he was a lone wolf. It is not difficult to be a lone wolf on a thousand pounds a year, especially in a period when a pound still meant a lot of money; but the lone wolf needs must forego popularity. In the same fashion as he understood, yet did not comprehend, Browne's qualities and shortcomings, he could not acquiesce in his lack of popularity, yet he did nothing about it.

Because of his eccentricity many thought him downright funny. I spoke to men and women of Woodbridge who told me how their parents had amused them when they were children with stories about FitzGerald, and how the parents, as children, had run from him in fear. But not every one of them; above everything, there was no cause for laughter over his generosity and kindness of heart. Here are two letters which I received in September 1947 which speak for themselves. They both came from the Whitgift Foundation, Croydon. Here is the first:

As a Girl I knew Edward FitzGerald when he lived at Boulge Hall Woodbridge but that is many years ago. As I shall be 91 in a week or two— As school children we used to go to the Hall for treats— When King Edward was married the Hall was opened to all comers— We used to think he was a very escntrect old Gentleman but he was a very good man I beleave he done a good deal of good among the poor—

But leaveing home about twelve years old— I did not hear much about him—

I have a few verces bye my side about him which I like to read and wish I had more of them—

I am afraid this will not be of any help to you for what you want—

I have often told my Children about him and made them laugh how he use to go about his plad Shawll over his Shoulder— Excuse me righting as I like to hear his name Mention. I wish you may hear more— From Mrs. S. Parker.

That letter would have given FitzGerald pleasure. It gave me some since Mrs. Parker referred to the plaid shawl he wore. That plaid shawl was hotly denied by a recent biographer who in every way, including the shawl, tried to prove that FitzGerald was like any other sober gentleman, almost like the gentlemen who travel up daily to the City in pin-striped suits, and that, too, was the impression the visiting niece had tried to give me.

Mrs. Parker's daughter, signing herself M. L. Parker, wrote to me as follows:

163

It may interest you to know that my Mother was a young girl in the village of Bredfield where Edward FitzGerald resided. Mother remembers the school treats at Boulge Hall & his expressions were a little peculiar, & the plaid shawl which he wore was one of his features, which added charm & goodness to the surrounding village, & which will ever remain in the memories of those who knew him.

I cannot quite see how a plaid shawl could add charm and goodness to any village, but the letter shows that Mrs. Parker spoke well to her daughter of FitzGerald.

Lone or not lone, the friend of Tennyson, Carlyle, and Thackeray needed near friends at the Hall, the Cottage, Farlingay Hall, Market Hill, and Little Grange. It was not so easy to find local friends, friends one could visit with at short distance—hence the already mentioned Woodbridge Wits, among whom now Bernard Barton takes up a sinister importance.

Bernard Barton was the Quaker poet. As a Quaker he was probably a good Quaker, for in 1824 his Society raised twelve hundred pounds for his benefit; but as a poet he was no good. When one walks about the streets of Woodbridge, one somehow feels the presence of Bernard Barton and his daughter Lucy, whom FitzGerald married. One feels it more in winter, for neither of them belonged to the impetus of spring nor to the warmth of summer.

During winter afternoons and winter evenings a small town like Woodbridge can be rather mournful. Nowadays one mostly sees people queueing up for the Ipswich bus or the bus that goes to Saxmundham; and the youth of the town loiters either at the Cross Roads, where Thoro'fare, Cumberland Street, and Church Street meet, or, which is more likely, outside the cinema beside the station. But, in your imagination, clear the town of queueing people, with women predominating, and of the cinema with uncouth boys loitering, and then there remains the drab, gray, silent provincial evening wherein moved the Bartons, father and daughter, equally drab and gray.

Therein they moved, schemed, and lived. On the other side of the same picture was FitzGerald with parrot, nasturtiums, toasted cheese, Aeschylus, and Calderón. And down beside the Deben, with the warehouses, the pub, and the old mill, one can almost see Lucy's ungainly gait, for it was there they saw each other for the last time, and FitzGerald, from the depth of the misery she had unsparingly given him, said to Posh: "Come on." In vain had she, the well-mannered lady, taken off her glove at the sight of her husband; probably that was all she ever took off in life.

Her father, Bernard Barton, came from Cumberland stock. He was of yeoman descent, but his grandfather, in deference to the trend of his age, became a calico printer. His claim to fame was a piece of machinery he had invented which "was so contrived that should any accident happen to one, the motion of that might be stopped without any impediment to the others." It also enabled twelve little girls to be spinning at once.

His son, Bernard Barton's father, was, according to Bernard Barton, of a literary turn of mind. He read Locke, Pope, and Addison. In spite of his reading and literary ambitions, he went to London where he entered the same sort of business he had left behind in the North —a wise precaution. In 1784 Bernard Barton was born and his mother died when he was only a few days old. The same was to happen to his daughter Lucy.

He spent his early years mostly with an uncle at Tottenham and went to a Quaker school in Ipswich. At the age of fourteen he was apprenticed to Samuel Jesup at Halstead in Essex. In 1806 he took himself to Woodbridge; a year later he married Lucy, Samuel Jesup's daughter, and with his brother-in-law started a corn and coal business. Lucy was born, his wife died, Barton left the business—according to FitzGerald "perhaps sickened with the scene of his blighted love,"—and became a tutor in a Liverpool merchant's house. He stayed there only one year; by the end of the year he must have overcome the blighted love, for he returned to Woodbridge and became a clerk in Messrs. Alexander's bank.

That small, insignificant post he managed to hold till his death.

He was not wholly unsuccessful in matters of money. He had received a donation from his Society, he got a pension of one hundred pounds a year from the Queen on Peel's recommendation when Peel left office, and FitzGerald helped him to the tune of three hundred pounds a year. Why Barton, the humble bank clerk, needed all that money is not known. Perhaps he did not, after all, drink only "a temperate allowance of generous port." Besides being a bank clerk, a poetaster, a financial wizard, he was also a persistent letter writer. He wrote diligently and he had to write often before an answer came. Nevertheless, he netted some good replies. Byron himself wrote him a letter; needless to say it was a reply.

"Having," wrote Byron, "your obliging expressions as to my productions for which I thank you very sincerely, and assure you that I think not lightly of the praise of one whose approbation is valuable: will you allow me to talk to you candidly, not critically on the subject of yours?"

He went on to say (the same advice Charles Lamb was to give him, too) that though Barton should not renounce writing, he ought not to trust entirely to authorship. On that first of June, 1812, Byron must have been in a remarkably good mood; he ended his letter to Barton with: "If others think as well of your poetry as I do, you will have no cause to complain of your readers."

The next feather in the industrious letter writer's cap was Southey. One surmises that Southey had been pestered a lot before he condescended to vouchsafe the information that he was a man of forty, younger in appearance than in habits, older in feelings and frame of mind, married for nineteen years, the father of seven children, two of whom, one his first-born, were in a better world. "You call me a fortunate being, and I am so, because I possess the will as well as the power of employing myself for the support of my family, and value riches exactly at what they are worth."

It is not difficult to visualize the effusive, humble, gushing letter which brought Southey's answer, the answer having begun as more or less all of Barton's correspondents began: "I should have answered your letter immediately if I had not been engaged with visitors when it arrived." And one feels that even Southey would not have been so pompous and conceited as to say, "But my wishes are bounded by my wants, and I have nothing to desire but a continuance of the blessings which I enjoy," had it not been in reply to an effusive, humble, and gushing letter.

When, in 1814, Barton published his *Metrical Effusions,* a copy was sent to Southey, who once more had to apologize for not having answered sooner. That time it was the slowness of the carrier. Then he proceeded to cheer up the author of *Metrical Effusions* with a few lines about Wordsworth, who lived fifteen miles from him.

"In conversation," he said of Wordsworth, "he is powerful beyond any of his contemporaries; and as a poet, I speak not from the partiality of friendship, nor because we have been so absurdly held up as both writing upon one concerted system of poetry, but with the most deliberate exercise of impartial judgment whereof I am capable, when I declare my full conviction that posterity will rank him with Milton."

It was kind of Southey not to tell Barton with whom he, the Quaker poet, would rank in time to come.

Southey on October 25, 1820, imparted the interesting piece of literary news that he had been commissioned to collect and arrange material for "the Life of George Fox and the Rise and Progress of the Quakers." Filled with enthusiasm, Barton was ready to help, but Southey found a helper nearer to Keswick. Barton shortly after sent him his "Day in Autumn" and again the carrier's wagon traveled so slowly that eighteen days had to elapse before receipt of the poem was acknowledged. Two months later another poem was sent to Keswick.

"Your poem," said Southey, "is a very pleasing one. How came the prejudice against verse to arise among

Quakers when so many of the primitive Quakers wrote verses themselves? Miserable bad ones they were but still they were intended for poetry."

Delighted, the Quaker poet sat down and sent more of his verses.

In Charles Lamb, however, he found a true friend. It is not because of Barton that I dislike Lamb. To me he seems too facetious, too light and easy—in short, a vulgarian. Though he wrote pleasingly and with charm, one feels that his tiny back was turned on the aristocratic eighteenth-century tradition; he was one of the advance party of the middle-class nineteenth century, fresh as the new paint on a new gate. He and Barton got on well. They must have made facetious jokes together.

After Elia's and Barton's deaths, Lucy, who had forsaken her father's faith and embraced the better-bred Anglican creed, called one day on Mary Lamb. Mary looked at Lucy's modest but un-Quakerish finery, then exclaimed reproachfully, "Bernard Barton's daughter!" Evidently it had been a family friendship.

To Lamb, as to Byron and Southey, Barton put the question whether or not he should remain a bank clerk. The idea of launching himself on the world as an unaided poet was often with Barton. He liked to fancy himself far from the madding desk but, apart from the importance he tried to attach in his letters to such a momentous parting of ways, he did nothing to implement it. Anyway, it did make him look daring in his own eyes. Lamb's answer was unequivocal.

"Keep to your bank," he wrote, "and the bank will keep you. Trust not to the public: you may hang, starve, drown yourself for any thing that worthy personage cares. I bless every star that Providence, not seeing good to make me independent, has seen it next good to settle me upon the stable foundation of Leadenhall. Sit down good B.B. in the banking office. . . ."

"Charles Lamb," said FitzGerald, "advises after his usual fashion: some grains of sterling available truth amid a heap of jests."

When the same question was put to Southey the answer was equally practical, though from another angle. He exhorted Barton to go early to bed; if he ate supper, to rest afterwards, but never compose, because one should go to bed with a quiet intellect, which is an intellectual as well as a religious peace of mind. Thus well-advised, Barton stuck to the ledger which, to judge from the spate of his verses, interfered little with his poetical work.

Besides his pension and his distinguished correspondents, Barton was not altogether without fame. A vessel on the Deben was named after him; and a niece once wrote to say that she had heard from her Aunt Lizzy that in Paris, at the theater where an English troupe was performing, and the name of one of the actors was Barton, the audience called out to ask if it were the Quaker poet himself.

Barton was as fond of pictures as FitzGerald, though even FitzGerald had to admit that Barton's knowledge of and taste in pictures were poor. In spite of that, they corresponded eagerly on painting. FitzGerald could be quite blunt about his friend's approach to pictures. He wrote to Barton from London in February 1842:

Your reason for liking your Paul Veronese (what an impudence to talk so to a man who has just purchased a real Titian) does not quite disprove my theory. You like the picture because you like the verses you once made upon it: you associate the picture (naturally enough) with them: and so shall I in future, because I like the verses too. But then you ask further, what made you write the verses if you were not moved by the picture imprimis? Why you know the poetic faculty does wonders, as Shakespeare tells us, in imagining the forms of things unseen, etc., and so you made a merit where there was none: and have liked the merit ever since. But I will not disturb you any further in your enjoyment: if you have a vision of your own, why should I undo it?

FitzGerald did not, one is given to believe, appreciate the lines on Paul Veronese as much as he politely said, for he ends the same letter with:

SONNET ON MY NEW PICTURE

. . . .
> Oh Twilight! Twilight! !

Rot me, if I am in a poetical humour: I can't translate the picture into words.

Bernard Barton could translate anything into words. His poetry had a wide range—quite unpalatably so. A couple of examples should suffice. The first verse of his poem "Autumn" clearly shows what he was capable of doing.

> *When is the aspect which nature wears*
> *The loveliest and dearest? Say it is in Spring,*
> *When its blossoms the apple-tree beauteously bears,*
> *And birds on each spray are beginning to sing?*
> *Or is it in Summer's fervid pride,*
> *When the foliage is shady on every side,*
> *And tempts us at noon in the green-wood to hide,*
> *And list to the wild birds warbling?——*

Of course, the loveliest and dearest aspect of nature, as the title implies, is autumn. The poem was composed in the grounds of Martin Cole, Esq., but that does not add to the luster.

He was prepared for every occasion. If a friend went to the seaside, rhymes would follow him:

> *Since Summer invited you to visit once more*
> *The haunts that you love upon Ocean's cool shore,*
> *Where billows are foaming and breezes are free,*
> *Accept at our parting a farewell from me.*

Now the question arises, how could FitzGerald have become Barton's friend? I seem to find a part of the answer in winter evenings in the empty streets of Woodbridge. From Barton's point of view it is simple enough. His company in Woodbridge would normally have consisted of the lawyer, the wine merchant, the better-off grocers, and, perhaps now and then, a clergyman. This last is, however, doubtful, considering that Barton was a Quaker. For him, therefore, to meet Mary Frances's son, the brother of the future squire of Boulge, was a great moment for which he must have striven a long time (they met in 1838). And then to discover that young Mr. FitzGerald was a lover of the arts too was simply sublime. The social advantage of FitzGerald's relationship with the Barton family should be stressed; it explains a lot. Yet it is quite as important to stress that, good poet or bad, Barton was a poet and, as Peel's care for Barton shows, poets in those days still had a position in the world. Their material betters had not yet ousted them.

The rest of the answer lies in the fact that on one side was FitzGerald, with his lonely, clinging soil at Boulge, and on the other Barton, with his mournful, cobbled winter streets. In Woodbridge Barton was probably the best talker; moreover, he had a quality which is always of help when dealing with one's superiors, namely he was not prone to take offense.

When, for instance, he sent Lamb a *Year Book* as a present, Lamb could, without fear of giving offense, tell him, "for God's sake do not let me be pestered with Annuals."

So FitzGerald and Barton became friends in quiet, uneventful, gossipy Woodbridge; and once you were FitzGerald's friend, all you had to do was to sit back and accept his devotion. That Barton did to his own advantage. Lucy was his only child. She began life with several handicaps. She was an ambitious girl but only the daughter of a bank clerk, though daughter of a poet too (a poet was still a fine romantic person even if most of that poet's time was spent behind somebody else's desk). It is unlikely that the local gentry fraternized with her. To ask her father, the poet, here and there was one thing, but toward the family, that is to say, toward Lucy, there was no obligation. The caste system in rural England was still a row of strong barriers; social conventions meant almost more than the change of seasons, for the seasons could change, whereas the rules that governed the gentry were and would remain, as far as the gentry knew, stable forever.

Lucy was too clever and too ambitious to settle down into Woodbridge middle-class life. The daughters of better-off tradesmen could be no companions for her. She was, after all, a poet's daughter and poets were the equals of princes. To begin with, she rid herself of the "thee" and "thou" of Quaker life. Barton acquiesced: it must handsomely be admitted that he was tolerant. He had a good word even for the Papists.

Given the circumstances in which she lived, there were two openings only for her desire to shine in the world. The first was to be worthy of the celebrated father, and the second charity and good works. These might help to jump the barriers of provincial life. To be worthy of her father meant to become a woman of culture; that she achieved up to a point. To have known Charles Lamb was in itself a hallmark of culture. Charity and good works were represented by the Bible class for boys which she held in her father's house every Sunday afternoon. She also taught at the village of Debach, a mile or so from Boulge, where FitzGerald came to help her now and then.

Their relationship was quite triangular—the small house in Woodbridge with the father and friend talking and the genteel, ugly Lucy listening, approving, and probably toasting cheese for them. There was, however, in the distance a keen observer: W. B. Donne. He met Barton through FitzGerald, and Barton began to correspond voluminously with Donne. Donne's letters to Barton were friendly but, like most of Barton's correspondents, Donne had often to apologize for not having answered sooner. Donne had a deep affection for FitzGerald. In almost every letter he wrote to Barton, FitzGerald was mentioned. FitzGerald appears to have been the one link between them. He wrote to Barton in the still happy Browne days:

I heard from Edward FitzGerald a few days since. He is leading his usual philosophic life in London, i.e. taking everything easily and making the most of whatever comes his way, which if not philosophy is something quite as good. Some time since, not being an angler himself, and not particularly affecting the company of rivers and standing pools, he nevertheless struck up an acquaintance with one who occupies himself by such waters: and this amphibious friend proves from his accounts to be one of the most agreeable acquaintances possible. He has had him in London, introducing him probably to the Paddington canal and serpentine, and pointing him out to the humane society as a person that should be looked after.

Urbane, kindly Donne and dear handsome Browne are warming flames in comparison to father and daughter in the Woodbridge house. "I may I trust," the father would write to Donne, "hope to hear from thee: that would be something to corroborate my vision of Mattishall. I must to my figures to sober myself." The figures were in Messrs. Alexander's bank.

It is FitzGerald who walks through the pages of Barton's and Donne's letters and without him, one feels, Donne and Barton would have had little to say

to each other. If FitzGerald is at Boulge, Donne en-
closes a note for him in the letter he writes in answer
to one of Barton's. If the note cannot be delivered then
Barton should put it into the Boulge letter bag, for
then it will be forwarded to him free. When Barton
can give news of FitzGerald he does so at once.

"Edward FitzGerald left Boulge Tuesday last for
Geldeston, proposing to go thence for Norwich with
the express desire of beating up thy Norwich Quar-
ters." On another occasion one hears a sinister ring;
while Barton writes to Donne, Lucy and FitzGerald are
left alone in the next room.

One wonders what Lucy and FitzGerald spoke of
when thus left alone. He probably did most of the
talking: of pictures, books, his London friends, never
for a moment dreaming that his friend's gaunt daughter would become one day his wife. She must have con-
versed of her Bible class and the school at Debach. Also
she could quite well relate her first meeting with Lamb.

Lucy was susceptible to FitzGerald's presence. True,
FitzGerald came mostly for her father's sake, but that
for Lucy was only the beginning. She had a high opinion of herself, and a high opinion, too, of the mission
of womanhood. Because she was ugly to look at she
cherished her mind and soul. She could not be blind
to the worldly side of the picture. Mr. Edward was the
son of Mrs. FitzGerald who lived at Boulge Hall—and

in other Halls, too—who drove about in a four-in-hand and ate off gold plate. The calico printer's grand-daughter, the bank clerk's child, was certainly impressed. To dream of being married to Mr. Edward was Cinderella's dream over again.

It could be said that a person like Lucy, without any physical attraction, without grace and social position, should not have dreamed of the eligible bachelor; but, in fact, she did. Hers were dreams of glory, almost of broken barriers. To be able to dine with the admiral's widow and the titled brewer, and to show off her learning, which consisted of knowing by heart her father's lines, was quite irresistible; but to achieve all that she must indeed become Mr. Edward's bride.

Some time before I decided to write of FitzGerald I was in a second-hand book shop in Colchester. The routine of second-hand book shops—the taking down of books without wishing to buy them or even to look seriously at them—prompted me to take down a volume which, as the title implied, had something to do with Suffolk. The title page was missing and what pages there were were badly foxed. The book contained a chapter on Woodbridge and, as I was living at Woodbridge, or rather near by, I looked through the chapter. Though the book had been written around 1860, the author had already cause to grumble at the narrowness of Thoro'fare. After a short description of the town he proceeded to praise the late Bernard Barton to whom, according to the author, the town owed its fame. He mentioned his excellent daughter Lucy who, so he put it, after her distinguished father's death married a Suffolk country gentleman.

The name of the country gentleman seemed of no importance to him, but somebody who had read the book—in fact, somebody in the know—had written on the margin of the page the name of Edward Fitz-Gerald. There then, long before I entered the old room, I knew that the important aspect of FitzGerald in the eyes of the world of his day was the fact that he was a country gentleman. Let it be added for Lucy's sake that the country gentleman's literary taste and cultured mind did add to the attraction; yet add only they did.

For Lucy not to think of FitzGerald's position in the county was, at the time, impossible. Even long after her time, conventions in Suffolk were quite rigid. A woman I know came as a young bride into Suffolk in the late nineties and she and her husband went to live in a hall which her father-in-law owned. I know the house; nowadays a drive connects it with the main road. But it was not so when she and her husband took up residence. It was the first afternoon, the sun shone and, looking out through a first-floor window, she saw a landau approaching across the heath. Beside the coachman sat the footman; the landau bumped and shook, and the branches of the trees played havoc with the footman's hat. Her first callers: she ran and changed and by the time the pitching landau had stopped before the entrance, she, dressed for the occasion, was awaiting her callers in the drawing room.

The point here is that nobody who went about with landau and footman called on the bank clerk's daughter. Were she, however, Mrs. FitzGerald, the landaus would come, heath or no heath. It is out of the question for Lucy not to have had that in mind.

Certainly with Mary Frances alive, stately and haughty, such dreams were of the futile kind. It is again Donne who sums up FitzGerald's relationship with his mother for my purpose. He tells J. W. Blakeley of FitzGerald:

He is more of a philosopher than ever, and his proficiency appears in wearing a most venerable coat and clouted shoon. He was when he left me, under marching orders for Hastings to convoy certain sisters. He has none of the inconveniences of marriage even in his state of innocence—and among them I should reckon not the least that of accompanying Mrs. FitzGerald [Mother] the round of the theatres to see the "Demon Dwarf" and sometimes Melodramas.

Lucy knew that FitzGerald was mother-ridden and in many ways sister-ridden; that, however, did not

181

worry her much. The mother would not live forever and, if one pursued the right policy, the sisters could be made harmless. That is understandable; many women have to face a similar problem. But to have imagined that a man like FitzGerald could be persuaded to lead the social life of a country gentleman is downright stupid. He had given it up long before Lucy began to hanker after it. Yet she persisted, eventually ruining everything. But for the time being, Mary Frances was still alive, and Lucy had to bide her time as patiently as she could.

FitzGerald would come and go and then absent himself from Suffolk for quite a while. Donne would try to persuade him to spend the winter in Dereham, but FitzGerald preferred his hated London. During his absence, Lucy and her father, rooted to Woodbridge, would wait for his return, the father writing letters and jingles, the daughter looking after him and teaching on a Sunday.

When Lucy was young there were no young men to court her: her male acquaintances were friends of her father. Hers was as drab an existence as only a small town can offer, and she hardened with the years. Excitements were few, one of them being the new ship called the *Bernard Barton* of which, with insight worthy of respect, her father said: "If my Bardship never gets me on the Muster-roll of Parnassus, it will into the Shipping-List!"

When FitzGerald, who was supping with them, was told of the ship, he jumped up, took his chair to the far corner of the room, and said he could not presume to sit at the same table with one about to have a ship named after him. Barton was delighted and Lucy must have smiled condescendingly. Jokes were in her line.

Barton glowed in FitzGerald's and Donne's friendship. Once, when FitzGerald was staying with Donne, the two of them decided to write a joint poem to Barton. The plan pleased them, and then, because FitzGerald was lazy, nothing came of it. The smallest tidbit about Donne or FitzGerald was of lasting interest to Barton. If FitzGerald disliked one of Donne's pictures, Donne knew that Barton would be glad to hear of it. Barton almost becomes likable because of the interest he took in his friend and patron's doings.

Donne wrote to Barton in June 1840:

Can you put a little ratsbane in E.FG.'s toasted cheese—not enough to make it fatal, but purely purgative. He has used me vilely. First he takes me to task for using long words, such as he says he does not understand: and then when I protest against being accused of affectation he defends himself by saying that I am not so much affected as stupid. "Shall this fellow live?" All authors are in danger from him, and should unite against him. And you have such an opportunity, as does not fall to every one's lot of quieting him.

Indeed, Barton's opportunities were many, for when FitzGerald was at the Cottage he saw Barton practically every day. Lucy, needless to say, was always present, but as yet not showing her hand. It is food for speculation as to whether, when he was not with them, but away in London in a world which was beyond Lucy's ken, it ever occurred to her that there was a side to the devourer of toasted cheese with which she had simply nothing to do. It is doubtful, however, that such thoughts ever came to her. She had no temperament and, consequently, little imagination. Also, she was of great patience: nothing could hustle her. On the other hand, for Prophecies and such-like matters she had a true regard. John, Edward's brother, was at Boulge Hall with his first wife in the summer of 1844, and gave, at the Woodbridge theater, a series of lectures on "The Prophecies." Barton did not go to them, but Lucy went and enjoyed them thoroughly.

Her doting father had to admit that she had a bee in her bonnet concerning the literal interpretation of Prophecy and divers Elysian crotchets on the subject of the Millennium. A pleasing thought to conjure up: the gaunt virgin, flushed with the vision of the Millennium, which, had it come in her time, she would not likely have endured.

On John FitzGerald's lectures, Donne commented as follows:

But the Woodbridge conversion of a Play-house into a house for the exposition of the Prophecies is the most remarkable diversion of a building from its original destiny I have ever heard or read of. Irving proved more than he dreamt of when he showed in the *Morning Watch* that the Apocalypse was a Drama in seven acts and that Jeremiah was a dramatic dialogue with lyrical choruses. I am afraid Miss Barton will consider me a profane person. . . .

Naturally, John FitzGerald's lectures in the theater did not appeal to the future Examiner of Plays.

John FitzGerald in those days was still under the influence of Preacher Matthews, for whom FitzGerald had a deep respect, too. Religion, for FitzGerald, was often a matter of caprice, but Lucy took hers as seriously as she took everything else. It is at moments difficult to imagine her sitting in the theater, listening to the rantings of Brother John who rolled his eyes and, when emotion shook him, made all sorts of faces and noises. Because it is difficult to imagine her listening to John's preaching, one cannot rid oneself of the suspicion that it was not only the Millennium that drove her to the theater but the desire, too, to ingratiate herself with the future squire of Boulge, who was to be the head of the family once Mary Frances died, an event decidedly this side of the Millennium.

Barton's health began to fail, chiefly because he took no exercise. Lucy should have nagged him into it in the same manner she later nagged her husband into dressing for dinner, but set dinners were of more interest to her than exercise. The county ladies hunted and went out with the guns; the bank clerk's daughter did nothing of the sort. So it is conceivable that, having no knowledge of exercise, it did not occur to her that her father led an extremely unhealthy life. Nevertheless, to spend a fine Good Friday with FitzGerald at the Cottage, her father waded through the melting snow; and I, who for my sins know what melting snow on clay soil is like, can but sympathize with him. Still there was, at the end of his wading, the reward of Fitz-Gerald's company, salt fish with egg sauce, and roast wild duck. As it was Good Friday, FitzGerald ate only fish; the Quaker poet enjoyed his duck.

Whether Lucy's future was mentioned when the two of them spent a long day together is not known. Tradition has it that it was only just before his death that Barton asked FitzGerald to look after his daughter. Tradition in this instance is quite untrustworthy.

Barton knew he possessed practically nothing in the world. After his death the pension would cease and Lucy, apart from the little house, would be left practically destitute. Barton was not without cunning, and one can almost see him walking beside FitzGerald in the slush, replete with duck, speaking of his Lucy and what would become of her after his death. FitzGerald, who had already given Barton plenty of money, probably answered without much thought that he would, of course, help her. Lucy could get the same help from him that the father had enjoyed. The idea that such help would entail marriage with the unattractive spinster simply could not have occurred to him. It was Lucy alone who interpreted it later as such. For Barton surely the thought that the rich, well-bred FitzGerald should ever contemplate marrying his daughter was, as Johnson had it, beyond his dreams of avarice.

On that Good Friday, the Boulge parson being ill, FitzGerald decided to go to evening service in Woodbridge. With Doubting Castle for the evening shelved, he stayed the night in Barton's house. There, in one room, FitzGerald slept with Calderón and Aeschylus, and Browne, too; in another room Lucy dreamed of her Millennium with landaus and rigid dinner parties.

The following Christmas he also stayed with the Bartons. Some time before he had been to London, which had inspired him with these lines:

In Craven Street, Strand, six attornies find place,
And six dark coal Barges are moored at its base;
Fly, Honesty, fly,—seek some safer retreat
For there's Craft in the river, and Craft in the street.

Barton was engaged on something important. Having been granted permission, he wrote some verses entitled "A New-Year Offering for the Queen." After that, slyly, pretending to be joking, Barton now and then expressed the hope that when Wordsworth died he might become the Laureate. Lucy, as a Christmas present, knitted a silk purse for FitzGerald, so Christmas, what with the verses for the Queen and the silk purse, was a cheerful one; but FitzGerald lost the purse straightaway.

Very likely in view of the Laureateship, Barton decided to have his portrait drawn by Samuel Laurence, the painter, who was FitzGerald's friend and correspondent. Barton much enjoyed sitting for Laurence, who had come to Woodbridge. While Laurence drew her father, Lucy sat in the corner of the room knitting, and FitzGerald sat with her reading the *Pickwick Papers*. Of the drawing, Barton said that Lucy was perfectly satisfied with it and that his friend Churchyard thought it admirable. Laurence charged fifteen pounds and poor Lucy paid out of her own purse.

Lucy was by then, as the standards of her time had it, a middle-aged woman without fortune or looks. The core of her virginity had hardened and the father had certainly given up all hope of her finding a husband. Apart from versifying he was an indolent man. His life consisted of sitting in the bank, now and again sitting under a tree, but mostly sitting at home. He was as much attached to his small comforts as to his gushing pen. For such a life a good housekeeper was essential. Lucy fulfilled the requirements and, it seems to me, Barton was utterly satisfied with his daughter's spinsterhood. If after his death FitzGerald would support her, then that was all to the good, and had he known that after his death his daughter would force FitzGerald into marrying her, he would have been delighted with that, too. Fundamentally, however, his pen and comforts were what mattered.

Surely in the dreary intimacy of long provincial evenings Lucy mentioned to her father her dreams and Millennium. The idea must have pleased him, and then he sat down and wrote to Donne: he was shocked because Donne had been to London to hear Jenny Lind sing. Meanwhile the Bartons' hold on FitzGerald strengthened: "Edward slept here last night and left us for Ipswich this morning. He returns from thence I think on Monday, as his Father is expected next week to stop a fortnight at Boulge." Barton wrote another dozen poems but, "I have not shown them either to Lucy or Edward—so they are as yet uncriticized."

To have his products criticized by FitzGerald, take his advice humbly, then do nothing about it was one of the pillars of their friendship. FitzGerald was deeply attached to him. There was so much love in Fitz-

Gerald that an outlet for it was continuously needed. Had he been a worldly man, like Thackeray, he could have spread it out; but as he was not, the small group around him received the full blast and sunshine of his affection.

Here Suffolk looms up again, with the encompassing sea, the trees, and the pale, wind-driven sky; and one knows that, looking at the wet clay and noisy swaying trees, it was a heartening thought for Fitz-Gerald to know that a few miles away there was a man whose leisure was entirely at his disposal, and who was, after all, a cultured man, interested in matters of the mind and the written word.

"The actual incidents," Barton frankly said, "of my life, to be sure, have been very few, but I have read, and thought and observed what has been going on around me, tolerably for a desk-bound wight. . . ."

Barton knew that he was a bad poet. FitzGerald admired him for that, but it was not difficult to get Fitz-Gerald's admiration, provided one was a friend. The admiration, however, was strictly limited to personal qualities. About his friends' works he could be scathing and, as was the case with Alfred Tennyson, often harsh and unjust.

In January 1849, a Mr. Vernon wrote to Barton asking him to furnish a preface to a book of poetry dedicated to the Earl of Carlyle. Barton declined in verse:

> *Used up! worn out! limping on my last legs!*
> *Alike unfit to teach the world—or learn!*
> *Draining life's mingled goblet to its dregs!*
> *Waiting in Charon's boat to take my turn!*

Barton died the following month, and a fortnight after his death FitzGerald wrote to Donne, telling him his friend had left little of worldly goods behind—

and we do not yet know what Miss B. will have or what else she is to do with herself. I (who was to go to Norfolk a fortnight ago) have waited here, looking over his papers, letters etc. more because it amused her, poor thing, to turn over all these things with one so intimate with her father, than for any good that can come of it. There are letters from C. Lloyd, Mitford, Southey etc. but no great shakes: and B.B.'s life would scarce make a thread to hang them on, even if they were available in other respects.

Eventually it was decided that a selection of Barton's works should be published with FitzGerald writing the Memoir. But what is interesting is FitzGerald's reference to Lucy as "poor thing." The woman one would consider marrying is hardly described or thought of as a poor thing.

Selections from the Poems and Letters of Bernard Barton, Edited by His Daughter, leave one quite unmoved; the Memoir on the other hand is perhaps Fitz-

Gerald's best bit of prose writing. The beauty and balance of his style shines forth; his control and choice of words is excellent. His honesty is apparent, too. However much he cared for Barton, however much he wished to please the bereaved daughter, he could not close his eyes to Barton's poor talent:

He wrote always with great facility, almost unretarded by that worst labour of correction; for he was not fastidious himself about exactness of thought or of harmony of numbers, and he could scarce comprehend why the public should be less easily satisfied. . . . No doubt he also liked praise; though not in any degree proportional to his eagerness in publishing; but inversely rather. Very vain men are seldom so careless in the production of that from which they expect their reward.

I do not think that Lucy was pleased with the Memoir. Her father had been, in her eyes, practically the greatest poet in the world. Even at the end of her long life, she was prouder, in the literary sense, of being Bernard Barton's daughter than of being Mrs. Edward FitzGerald. She must have argued with FitzGerald, asking him to delete this, omit that; but in matters of taste and conscience one could not argue with him. Neither was she in the exact position where arguing is its own reward. He knew better than she how to make the selections, his purse was at her disposal, and the FitzGerald family handsomely subscribed to the work:

Mary Frances, ten copies; John, one; Peter, four; and Edward, ten. Yet the most important thing for Lucy was that FitzGerald had without a murmur, almost automatically, undertaken to look after her. Her dying father had asked him to do so, and now it all was as she precisely wished it. That for her was the first step.

The point which strikes one as odd is that the marriage did not come about till seven years later. The explanation is simple: Mary Frances was still alive. Lucy, under that formidable shadow, could not force the issue; besides, she was a patient woman. Mary Frances died on January 30, 1855, and it was only in the following year that Lucy forced Mary Frances's son to marry her. It is conceivable that, having lost his overbearing mother, FitzGerald wished to replace her with another overbearing woman. That idea can be dismissed. Whereas mothers are not chosen but loved, with wives it is often the other way round. What I feel happened was that Lucy blackmailed FitzGerald into marriage by telling him that her position was compromised because she was being kept by a man who was not her husband.

That is quite monstrous. She had used his kindness as a lever for blackmail and, since of love she had none for him, the excuse that all is fair in love cannot be applied. She was a grim woman, nearly fifty years old at the time of their marriage. But she knew her

FitzGerald well. She played on his respect for the forlorn damsel, brought her hard weapon to bear on his sense of chivalry, and, once chivalry had been set in motion, knew she was the winner. It is good to think that hers was a truly Pyrrhic victory, but she brought FitzGerald endless misery.

She was a woman of acute limitations and not of the great world. Neither was FitzGerald of the world, but by birth and upbringing that world was his and it was his business whether he renounced it or not. For her the social world was the goal; for him it was something which he did not particularly like. She thought, because hers was a limited, insensitive brain, that she could force the issue. Marriage she did succeed in forcing, but she was incapable of changing his way of life. The idea of chivalry and sacrifice could appeal to him; to wear an evening suit did not. She achieved what she thought important yet lost because she had not the gift to appreciate detail.

FitzGerald was also well in middle age at the time of their marriage. His crotchets were numerous, his mode of life had completely crystallized. He must have known that life with Lucy could not work. Still, the idea of sacrifice and the rescue of the aging, forlorn damsel had their morbid charm. Like most eccentrics, he stood in fear of conventions. They who break them must pay great attention to them. Browne advised him against the marriage and told him it would not work, he would be unhappy. FitzGerald countered with what would the world say.

"That from you!" said Browne. "*You* who do not care a straw what anybody says about anything."

"Nor should I care," said FitzGerald, "but Miss Barton would care a very great deal. It would be cruel."

To this, Browne had no answer.

There it was in a nutshell, and now I had better hand over to my strangers. I met the strangers in the Ipswich Public Library. Among the few papers there relating to FitzGerald, I found some sheets containing questions and answers. Who put the questions and who gave the answers, I do not know. Perhaps the questions were put by John Glyde, who wrote the first *Life of FitzGerald,* and the answers came from Spalding, of Colchester, who knew FitzGerald intimately. At any rate I like listening to distant voices without much bothering about their identity. Somehow it makes them more convincing. So, while the trolley buses passed, cars hooted, and a watery sun waited to give way to the rain which would beat down on the Orwell, I listened to the strangers.

Query: Bernard Barton died in 1849 but his daughter did not marry FitzGerald until 1856. A period of seven years thus elapsed between the marriage of the daughter and the death of the father. Why and where was Lucy Barton during that time?

Answer: I believe that L.B. lived in the family of the Gurneys in Norfolk, perhaps as friend or companion during that time.

Query: E.FG. was criticized for marrying L.B. and separating so soon. Reason for marriage? Each must have realized unsuitability. He made very handsome provision for her and appears to me to be most to be pitied. Courting during B.B.'s life as E.FG. was frequently in the house?

Answer: I don't think marriage was considered during B.B.'s life. B.B. very anxious as to L.B.'s future after his death. Believe E.FG. assured him she would be provided for.

Question: L.B.'s appearance?

Answer: Perhaps I never saw Mrs. FG. more than three or four times and never spoke to her. She was tall, rather masculine looking, and I think turning grey.

Query: Manners? Masterful in tone, low in voice, and all fussy in manners.

Answer: She used to stay with her old friend Mrs. Dr. Jones at Woodbridge. She seemed to me pretty portly, plain looking, and with rather masculine features. I never heard her speak. They were separated when I went to Woodbridge in August 1859.

Question: Walk? Peculiar walk, sort of stride that attracted attention?

Answer: I never noticed anything unusual in her walk.

Question: Dress? Quaker influence.

Answer: She dressed well but plainly. I should never have known her to be a Quakeress. (Of course she was not.)

Here for the time being I must leave the strangers but will return to them in FitzGerald's later years. It is difficult to visualize FitzGerald in the company of that portly, plain-looking woman with masculine features. He loved wild flowers, nasturtiums, the sunny Browne, but to love Lucy would have been a negation of all he believed. Nevertheless, if she had had any sense, she could in a fashion have made the marriage a success. There was no physical attraction on either side—it is almost quite certain that the marriage was never consummated—but FitzGerald was a good man, and had she shown any understanding or devotion, he would have settled down with her and she could have become a sort of sister, receiving all the brotherly affection he was capable of giving. And he could give a lot.

She had no sense, and thought, by forcing the issue, she would triumph. The first round, marriage, she had won, so why should she not succeed with the rest, the rest being FitzGerald's way of life?

After the *Selections* had been published, Lucy became companion to the daughter of Hudson Gurney of Keswick Hall, Norwich. She was eminently suited to hold a post like that. Norwich was only in the next county and, when Mary Frances died, she could return quickly enough. Meanwhile, she worked her legend. The legend was that FitzGerald, having been the executor of her father's will, discovered that her income was too small for her to live properly and had thought it his duty under the circumstances to ask her to marry him. He asked and she accepted. Therefore it was all of FitzGerald's doing.

Notwithstanding that after Lucy's death in 1898 (she outlived FitzGerald by some fourteen years), the Academy supported the legend, there is no truth in it. FitzGerald knew she would be poor long before her father's death; he was not the executor of the will; and if he had thought that she could live in ease only as his wife, then he would have proposed to her years earlier. No, it was Lucy who worked for the marriage, and the time of the marriage is also ample proof that it was her doing. FitzGerald had already supported her for seven years without her being his wife, so why should he have decided after seven years that it was preferable to turn the woman he was supporting and would continue to support into his wife? The legend does not work.

FitzGerald entered into marriage joylessly. He wrote

to tell Thackeray that he was getting married, and Thackeray wrote to John Allen saying, "E.FG. of course has written to you about his marriage. He ordered me not to congratulate him and I can only wish him good fortune. . . ." FitzGerald told Crabbe, too, that he was getting married and asked Crabbe not to congratulate him.

His friend Donne wrote to Fanny Kemble:

Edward FitzGerald is at this moment or in a very few days or hours will be—"Benedick the married man!" He is married or going to be married to Lucy Barton. *"Bélier, mon ami, vous me ferez grand plaisir si vous commencerez par le commencement."* Who is "Lucy Barton"? Lucy is the daughter of Bernard Barton, whilome Banker's clerk and poet at Woodbridge. She is about a year younger than her husband, consequently about 48: and in respect that she is tall and well filled out, Charles is wont to call her Barton-Barton, conceiving, I suppose, that Baden-Baden means double Baden.

Barton-Barton's wedding did not take place in Wood-bridge, the home of both parties, but at All Saints Church, Chichester, on November 4, 1856, and it is significant that not one member of the large FitzGerald family was present. On the other hand, FitzGerald was hemmed in by Bartons. It was the day of their glory: the bank clerk's daughter had made good. There were Emily Barton, Anne Barton, Elisabeth Barton, Joseph

Barton, and Gerald Barton. Surrounded by them, guarded by them, he became Lucy's husband. All Fitz-Gerald could say (so he had said to Spring Rice) was: *vogue la galère!* He walked beside her mute, his head bowed, and when at the wedding breakfast he was offered blancmange, virginal in color and heavy for the palate, he said in disgust: "Ugh! Congealed brides-maid!"

One is greatly indebted to Mr. Terhune for having recorded that sad, miserable exclamation.

And, "ugh" with his congealed wife, he moved to London after a few weeks in Brighton. They lived in Great Portland Place for some time. FitzGerald proba-bly imagined that the life she would care to lead would be similar to the life she had led in her father's house: housekeeping, Bible classes, reading and quiet. But that sort of life was good enough for a clerk's daugh-ter; Mrs. Edward FitzGerald must lead the life her station demanded of her. She soon began to nag him, to make life wretched for him. He should dress differ-ently, he should behave differently, and let his life be different, too. Of those days Sir Frederic Pollock, who visited them, left a moving picture:

. . . after his marriage when he was for some weeks in London in Portland Terrace, Regent's Park, he dined with us together with his wife and we took tea one afternoon with them. Both occasions were altogether uncomfortable ones and it was a relief when the evening at our home and the afternoon at his place came to an end. The wretchedness of the terrible mistake he had made was apparent all the time and on leaving his own place he came away with us very much the worse for some wine he had been taking, a condition in which I never saw him at any other time.

The months he spent with Lucy were like a drunken haze. After a while she departed for Norfolk, apparently looking for a suitable house for them. It is strange that she did not want to settle in or around their Woodbridge. She preferred Norfolk where, because of the time she had spent in the Gurney household, she had more distinguished acquaintances. He should have joined her in Norfolk; he did not. She came back to London and they removed to Portland Terrace. They remained in those lodgings for four months. Thackeray came to see him once. To see his old friend upset him greatly. There was much shilly-shallying about their eventual home. FitzGerald felt that Lucy should first find a house and, if it suited her, he would then decide whether it suited him, too.

In June, Donne reported to Fanny Kemble that "Fitzgerald [sic] has rejoined his better half and John Fitzgerald [sic] just hired a sixth house—less than half a dozen will not serve him to occupy at once. . . ."

It was easy for John to have six homes since he was devoted to his wife; but to his brother the idea of even one with Lucy had become repugnant. The forlorn damsel had turned into a nagging, pretentious bully, and chivalry withered in his heart. Drink is a good companion of self-pity. Lucy went again to Norfolk and stayed with friends at Garleston near Yarmouth. FitzGerald joined her. He cried out to his friend Cowell who had latterly gone to India: "To India! It seems to me it would be easy to get into the first great Ship and never see Land again till I saw the mouth of the Ganges! and there live what remains of my shabby life."

George Borrow lived not far from Yarmouth. He and FitzGerald were not good friends. The quietist and the exuberant were little drawn to each other. Nevertheless, Borrow paid FitzGerald and Lucy a visit. They drank, FitzGerald got drunk, walked home with Borrow (as with the Pollocks in London, anything was an excuse to be away from Lucy), and, coming back, lay down on the grass by the roadside and slept there till dawn. In August they separated.

Of the actual moment of separation hardly anything is known. An inquisitive person, years after FitzGerald's death, wrote to Aldis Wright, his literary executor, asking for details of the marriage and separation. He received a snorter but no information in reply. Thus their last days together are only a matter of conjecture. I believe it was he who forced the issue. Lucy was too stupid and too insensitive to see that her plans had miscarried. FitzGerald had become quite insufferable, yet, for a hard creature like Lucy, that was no reason to give up her hopes. Husbands who go off with departing guests, under the influence of drink, and spend the night on the wayside are no pillars of married life. Still, I feel it was FitzGerald who told her to go.

So they separated, and here one cannot resist reflecting that the man who had to marry, according to his own standards of chivalry, the woman he could not support otherwise in the world's eyes, parted from her after nine months of marriage without the slightest regard for Victorian squeamishness: an interesting reflection, partly revealing FitzGerald's inconsistency of sentiment and chiefly showing how wretched and miserable Lucy had made him. Though parted, he continued to provide for her handsomely: she could have all she wanted but not him. That, luckily, he retained for himself. Thus Lucy fades out and FitzGerald goes his own way toward the Sultan's turret which, by then, had begun to take shape.

FitzGerald's first biographer wisely sums up the marriage by saying that, whatever the final judgment is, those who have faith in FitzGerald need have no fear. Thomas Wright remarks: "How strange that everybody could love FitzGerald, put up with his peevishness and eccentricities, nay love him more for them, except one person—his wife!" His latest biographer, Mr. Terhune, however, considers that "a full share of the blame for the failure of his marriage should be heaped upon FitzGerald's head. . . ." With him one has to disagree.

FitzGerald, a fact Mr. Terhune often forgets, was a man of genius. Of geniuses, even at the best of times, there are too few in the world and the world does not suffer them gladly. In self-defense and self-preservation the genius must go his own way. If anybody wishes to travel with him, then it is for the fellow-traveler to make concessions, since, logically enough, the chosen road is not his. FitzGerald chose the road and Lucy, who had seen him on that road for many years before their marriage, can alone be blamed, for she had decided to join him on it. To us for whom, because of his genius, his life has become public property (only the undistinguished take their lives to the grave), his separation from Lucy is cause to rejoice. Had he succumbed to her petty whims, his flame would have turned into a small gray flicker and neither Mr. Terhune nor I should have found much to write about him.

She was a peevish creature with a small range of feeling. After the separation she finally settled down at Croydon, another small town, and, having outlived her husband, died in 1898, on the threshold of a century she would deeply have resented. Some time before she died, her landlord sold the house she lived in and she had to leave. It is recorded that when the news was broken to her, she was more distressed than she had been over her marriage, and moaned around, "Oh the old home, oh the old home."

Part Five

THE RUBÁIYÁT AND THE LETTERS

"THE MIGHTY generation of Poets which had just disappeared passed over the face of England like a thunderstorm." So lamented Taine. Keats, Shelley, and Byron were indeed like thunderstorms, glorious and wild, but of short duration. The poets who came after them were more like steady rain, which quite often revives the land just as well. Tennyson had that rain-like quality; so had Browning.

Notwithstanding his longevity, FitzGerald as a poet had the quality of which thunderstorms are made. For the effect of the Quatrains is still that of the thunderclap, despite the apparent contradiction that he worked on the Rubáiyát slowly and in a leisurely manner. It must be admitted that FitzGerald lives mostly by the Rubáiyát and the *Letters,* which are not read enough. Of his other works, *The Bird Parliament* is perhaps the best. He thought it was his best; but one is always exceedingly loyal to one's second best.

At first glance, one would say that his was not an independent genius. If one looks at his works rigidly, one can define them as translations, with the exception of *Euphranor*, which would not qualify him as a genius. Even *Euphranor* is crowded with quotations from other thinkers and writers, and most of the arguments are based on them. Yet, he was no true translator. His translations are not accurate, nor in all sincerity did he wish them to be so. One could say that other people's writings and thoughts were his inspiration and for this reason he should not be placed among the great who wrote and thought independently. That is, I think, an unfair argument.

No creative artist is independent. Inspiration comes from outside for the creative machinery to receive it.

The loss of his friend Hallam inspired Tennyson neither more nor less than Aeschylus inspired FitzGerald to render his *Agamemnon* into English. Once Arnold Bennett sat in a restaurant in Paris; an aging woman came in, and the sudden thought came to Bennett that that woman, too, had once been young. The thought enveloped the woman, and out of that reflection Bennett brought forth his best novel: *The Old Wives' Tale*. FitzGerald met Calderón, in the shape of his works, and out of that meeting rose the six translations. He was as little independent as other creative artists, the one conspicuous difference being that with him it was not the person nor the landscape which inspired him, not even the misery of others—only their writings.

He was, in his lazy fashion, something of a scholar. His daydreams consisted not of speculating on other people's vagaries and hidden lives but on the written word. His translations were not so much the desire to "english" foreign writers but to live with them, understand them, and recreate them in English, in the same way that Tennyson desired to recreate and understand King Arthur.

Here, once again, one must dwell on FitzGerald's financial independence. If he had had to earn his living, which he surely would have wished to earn from writing, would he have branched out as a poet and writer who took inspiration not from books but from life itself? He said he was a translator in no need of money; yet, had he been in need of earning a literary income, he might have translated more, he might have become a somewhat intolerant critic, but neither a Tennyson nor a Thackeray was lost in him because of his money. It was the written word that made him rejoice, and so it would have been under whatever conditions he had lived.

With that fact in mind, one can explain all FitzGerald's important big works except the Rubáiyát. That amazing meeting between FitzGerald and Omar Khayyám was like the wind-borne seed entering the waiting earth. About the seed there is little mystery, but why should the earth have waited?

Often on summer evenings, taking myself for a leisurely walk with my gun and the vague intention of shooting a rabbit for the dogs, I thought of FitzGerald and Omar Khayyám as you think of two men you see much together who puzzle you by the reason and force of their friendship. The land of Boulge around me was of little help. In '46 clouds hung heavily in the sky; the earth was wet and my boots in the clay made loud kissing sounds. The following year the sun was hot; the earth was like the hard wrinkles of an old woman; of the Rubáiyát there was nothing either in the wet or warm air. It would be better for the time being, I thought, to look only at FitzGerald's works and try to forget the man. That, I soon found out, was impossible.

Usually the working life of a writer is like a graph. He starts on high, slowly descends, and then it is said that he did not fulfill his promise. Or he may start low and work himself slowly up, in which case critics are much pleased with him. Or again—and this is the normal course—he keeps up a level till a certain age and then the downhill move begins. FitzGerald fits in nowhere. He had published *Polonius*, the first six dramas of Calderón, *Euphranor*, and *Salámán and Absál* before the Rubáiyát. After the Rubáiyát came two dramas of

Calderón, *Agamemnon, The Downfall and Death of King Oedipus, Readings in Crabbe,* and *The Two Generals*. Therefore, one sees no graph, hardly a chart: good, often pleasing, English renderings with *Agamemnon* at the top; yet they all seem quite unrelated to the warmth, the ecstasy and burning imagery of the Rubáiyát. Of course, it was the same FitzGerald behind all of them: leisurely, sensitive to words, not too accurate or conscientious, but it was not the burning FitzGerald, the Sappho of a much larger, chimney-clad island.

In his other writings the flame was of a quiet sort.

I think [he wrote], I want to turn his [Aeschylus's] Trilogy into what shall be readable English Verse: a thing I have always thought of, but was frightened of the Chorus. So I am now; I can't think them so fine as People talk of: they are terribly maimed: and all such Lyrics require a better Poet than I am to set forth in English. . . . I think I shall become a bore of the Bowring order, by all this Translation: but it amuses me without any labour, and I really think I have the faculty of making some things readable which others have hitherto left unreadable.

And so it was. His translations were readable, full of good taste and his own good mood. However, he did not feel with Calderón, nor was he altogether happy in ancient Greece. Calderón was a Spaniard, a courtier, and pious. Piety, FitzGerald understood up to a point, but a courtier was a man completely divorced from his own thoughts and way of life, and a Spaniard probably reminded him only of the ill-fated General Torrijos. Of the Greek translations it can be said that they were neither ancient nor modern and, as A. C. Benson put it, they were Greek plays only in the sense that the Eglington Tournament was a medieval joust. On the other hand, FitzGerald had adopted his own method and, at least, he stuck to it. Moreover, his life, his surroundings and pastimes were all such that accuracy little entered into them. He did miss the spirit of Classical Greece, but it was not a spirit he was fundamentally drawn to. He liked to be surrounded by it, not to enter it. But for his genius, his Greek and Spanish translations would have been the work of a cultured, well-to-do gentleman. But for his genius! Once one has it, one cannot get rid of it, as these words of Cassandra in *Agamemnon* show:

Oh,
a nightingale, a nightingale indeed,
That, as she "Itys! Itys! Itys!" so
I "Helen! Helen! Helen!" having sung
Amid my people, now to those who flung
And trampled on the nest, and slew the young,
Keep crying "Blood! Blood! Blood!" and none will heed!
Now what for me is this prophetic weed,
And what for me is this immortal crown,
Who like a wild swan from Scamander's reed
Chaunting her death-song float Cocytus down?

Whether Aeschylus truly moved him or not, the strong flow of his gift is with Cassandra. FitzGerald knew his own shortcomings and in his preface to *Agamemnon* he admits that "to recreate the Tragedy, body and soul, into English and make the Poet free of the language which reigns over that half of the world never dreamt of in his philosophy, must be reserved— especially the Lyric part—for some Poet, worthy of that name, and of congenial Genius with the Greek."

Walking along with my gun, I saw a rabbit disappear in a hedge. It suddenly occurred to me that if FitzGerald, who had so often walked along the same stream, were to come up behind me, and I were to ask him why it was that not Aeschylus but Omar Khayyám, the lecherous old drunk, was congenial to him, FitzGerald surely would have stared at me in amazement. For FitzGerald, with the exception of writing the Rubáiyát, never gave way, not even to himself.

My theory by then had more or less evolved. The repressed FitzGerald had found his sublimation in Omar Khayyám. What life did not give him, what he would not take from life was handed to him, through the centuries, by a man who, if they had met, would have filled him with disgust. FitzGerald took from the East what his Western soul unconsciously longed for. He did not wear Omar's rich garment; he cut it to his size. He wore it under the grey Suffolk sky, unaware that the same garment had been worn in the dusty street of the bazaar—a bazaar with camels just passing and, over there, a tavern with pretty young boys.

Theirs was a communion in which FitzGerald took all and Omar asked nothing, and that is why FitzGerald was able to give us not a Persian in heavy tweeds but himself in his own true colorful glory. To Omar had belonged FitzGerald's real self, but only so far as the real self is allowed to exist. The real self comes forth at odd moments and, if it does not retreat quickly enough, it becomes a bore both for owner and beholder. Napoleon's true self came out as the sun of Austerlitz rose; but how long did it take the sun to rise? Not long; and neither was the meeting between Omar and FitzGerald of long duration. But as the sun shone so briefly on Napoleon's victory over the two emperors, so Omar and FitzGerald had communed long enough for one of the masterpieces of the English language to be born.

For a masterpiece it undoubtedly is, and, walking beside the stream with my gun, I remembered that as a boy I had not been allowed to read it. When later on I asked why, the answer was that it was too sexy for a boy. Yet one cannot put a finger on that flow of sex with which the quatrains stream. It is Omar's, but longed for by FitzGerald. He went through life sexless but full of *Schwärmerei*. His loves were of the heart, and Thackeray, Browne, and Posh, though of the flesh, were but mates of his soul. The written word of Omar intoxicated his senses, and so again, as with his other works, we find him with the word and not with flesh and blood.

It should not be imagined that their meeting was like lovers finding each other in the night: quick and sharp. It was quiet and unhurried. FitzGerald did not sit up in the night, his brow glistening with perspiration, his feverish hand grabbing the pen as one grabs at the hand of the beloved. It was nothing of the sort; it took years, and continuous corrections followed, with FitzGerald leaving out this, adding that. It was discussed with friends, and now and then he left it alone altogether. The spark did not glow forth but was within him, where it leaped and burned, and at last appeared the quatrains, carefully polished. Love and joy are one thing, but to write and write well is another. To have lain, as it were, with Omar was of the flesh, but to translate him into words needed workmanship.

FitzGerald was a poet, and a great poet to boot; therefore, craftsmanship in the end almost overshadowed love and joy. Creation is bisexual. Vague figures asking for shape and form float over the darkness. The rising light embraces them and, still uncertain, they rise with it. It is the light which is also the word that gives them its own life, a life which is the contrast of darkness, and so the vague figures are at its mercy. But merciful, creation is: the figures move, they breathe, and now, all on their own, they separate from the light. Left to themselves, they move, they dance and weep. The light recedes, and it will be judged by the figures now rollicking with life. . . .

A rabbit came out of a hedge and I shot it. I picked up the rabbit and put it into the game bag. The communion, I thought, between the man of Suffolk and the Persian wizard was, naturally, not altogether smooth. There were many misunderstandings, the chief of which was that what seemed to FitzGerald like vice, despair, and passion, was for Omar the ordinary course of his Eastern existence. Omar was not as great a philosopher as FitzGerald believed him to be, nor such a fine poet. In Persia Omar hardly ranks with the giants, and, talking to educated Persians, I have reached the conclusion that the eternity of the Rubáiyát will be assured more by FitzGerald than by Omar, notwithstanding FitzGerald's misunderstandings and misinterpretations, which, however, from the artist's point of view, little matter. You can be a fine painter without taking into consideration the exact number of trees you see.

The agnostic who took the Rubáiyát for his anthem was, one feels, as mistaken as the man who tried to find the elegiac qualities of *Alice in Wonderland*, and of course he found them. The form and the intoxication of creating are paramount to the artist; it is left to the reader to find whatever he fancies; and, alas, one can trust the reader.

FitzGerald never saw the East, never wanted to see the East. He invented an East of his own into which the quatrains fitted. The streets in the bazaar would have shocked him because of their filth and noise. The streets he created would have been genteel, had not a FitzGerald he himself would not have recognized in real life walked through them. When Edward Clodd says, "Omar Khayyám has been dead nigh eight hundred years, but his words have not passed away. Roses still scatter their petals by his resting place," one has only to remember that there were no roses on Omar's grave. The entire idea of the Omar Khayyám cult would have surprised and probably pained FitzGerald. Nevertheless, it is important to examine Omar's life, even if cursorily, for Omar was the mainspring of the beauty in which, in his own fashion, with his own temperament and character, FitzGerald found his fulfillment.

Omar Khayyám's name was Ghiyas uddin Abul Fath Umar ibn Ibrahim al-Khayyámi, and the man should be referred to as Umar Khayyám; but, since it is as Omar Khayyám we know him in the West, it would be pedantry to speak of him as Umar, especially as FitzGerald knew and spoke of him as Omar. He was born in Nishapur in the province of Khorassán. The date of his birth is not known. He died around 1123 A.D. He was at the time of his death of great age. He was supposed to be a hundred, but in the East, once you are over fifty, you can, if you feel like it, call yourself a hundred years old. It is known, however, that when, in 1075, Malik-sáh established his observatory, Omar became employed there with Abu'l-Mudhaffar al-Isfizári and Maymún ibn Najib al-Wasítí.

His life is mostly legendary and most of the legends have by now been refuted, but it is possible that he was one of the Assassins. The oldest account of him is in the *Chahár Maqála*, in which he is mentioned only as an astronomer and astrologer. *Chahár Maqála* means "four discourses," and each discourse contains anecdotes. In Anecdote XXVII it is related that Omar had gone to the town of Balkh, into the street of the slave sellers, and there, in a friendly gathering, gave the Proof of Truth, saying his grave would be in a spot where the trees would shed their blossoms twice a year on him. And Didhámí, the author of the discourses, went to Nisha-pur in the year A.H. 530 (A.D. 1135–1136), the same year "the great man had veiled his countenance in the dust, and this lower world had been bereaved of him."

It was a Friday; he engaged a guide who took him to the tomb, which was at the foot of a garden wall. A peach tree and a pear tree thrust their heads over the wall and Didhámí remembered what Omar had said in Balkh; he broke down and wept, for "nowhere in all the regions of the habitable world had he seen one like unto him." He adds, however, that Omar had never believed in astrological predictions.

Omar was equally successful with another piece of prophecy, even if he did not believe in prediction. The king went hunting, but before going a-hunting, Omar had told him that on the day in question there would be neither snow nor rain. The king believed Omar till clouds began to gather; then he was less prone to heed his word. There came wind, snow, and mist and everybody laughed at Omar. But Omar knew what he had been talking about. Besides, it was too late to retract his words. He said to the king: "Have no anxiety, for this very hour the clouds will clear away and during these five days there will be not a drop of moisture."

The weather cleared, the king rode on, and Omar was once more successful with his prognostication. "But," adds the author, "prognostication by the stars, though a recognized art, is not to be relied on, and whatever the astrologer predicts, he must leave to Fate." Fate is very tangible in the East, and Omar must have left the success of his predictions to it with as much confidence as St. Ignatius in the West left his and his Order's success to the Mother of God.

How far Omar could have predicted the weather at Boulge is not even food for thought, but one believes that FitzGerald would rather have listened on that score to his old gardener, late of the Napoleonic wars.

Omar was, so the *Nuzhatu'l Arwáh* (Recreation of Souls) tells us, a follower of Avicenna, the mathematician, and he was ill-tempered and inhospitable. He was a favorite of the Sultan Maliksáh, and besides his astronomy, astrology, and mathematics, he was the inventor of a clay scarecrow. An amusing legend has it that a certain theologian who used to denounce him from the pulpit as an atheist and freethinker would come to Omar privately in the mornings to take lessons in philosophy.

Legends encompass him, the best-known one being the tale of Omar and his two friends, Nidhámu'l-Mulk and Hassan-iSabbáh, with whom he had been at school in Nishapur. Theirs was a devoted friendship, and when they parted they partook of each others' blood and swore a solemn oath that whichever of them should attain power would help the others. Nidhámu'l-Mulk became prime minister. Omar went to see him and very properly reminded him of the covenant of their youth. Said the prime minister: "I give thee the government of Nishapur and its dependencies."

Omar was no fool and preferred a pension which was paid to him annually, tax free.

FitzGerald knew this legend, and Omar's indolence, lack of wish for power, must have endeared the astronomer to him. Indolent though he was, like FitzGerald, Omar wrote a good deal. Ten works, including the Quatrains, are attributed to him; he also helped Maliksáh with his reformed calendar. His philosophy concerns us in a sense, but only as far as the Rubáiyát goes. Even with the little knowledge I have on the subject, Omar's philosophy seems often vague, confused, and perhaps he himself was pretty uncertain about it. Now and then, as a pupil of Avicenna, he would turn to God and say: "Verily I have striven to know Thee according to the range of my powers, therefore forgive me, for indeed such knowledge of Thee as I possess is my means of approach to Thee." In fact, those are attributed to be his last words. Other times he was the cynic, the debauched, and the blasphemer. Edward G. Browne, in his *Year Amongst the Persians,* quotes from Jamí's *Baharistan:*

> *O God, although through fear I hardly dare*
> *To hint it, all this trouble springs from Thee!*

That often was Omar's mood and the following lines of Jamí suited his mood, too:

> *Dead drunk, not like a common sot, one day*
> *Nasir-i-Khusraw went to take the air.*
> *Hard by a dung-heap he espied a grave*
> *And straightway cried, "O ye who stand and stare,*
> *Behold the world! Behold its luxuries!*
> *Its dainties here—the fools who ate them there!"*

Omar was at times a believer in the doctrine of metempsychosis. One day he was walking with a group of students outside the college where donkeys were bringing bricks. One of them, with true donkey stubbornness, refused to enter the college. Smiling broadly, Omar went up to the donkey and extemporized this quatrain:

> *O lost and now returned "yet more astray"*
> *Thy name from men's remembrance passed away,*
> *Thy nails have now combined to form hoofs,*
> *Thy tail's a beard turned round the other way!*

Not very tactful words, but the donkey entered the college; then Omar explained to the students that the ass in a former life had been a lecturer at the college and out of shyness would not go in. Since Omar recognized him, his former colleague, there was nothing else left for the ass to do but to enter the college.

The feeling that Omar's philosophy was based mainly on his indolence and love of the good things of life persists. The day was his and, according to the day, his thoughts varied. Fate was always present: it had not treated him badly and the luxury of thought and dream was, thanks to the stipend from his friend, the prime minister, quite undisturbed. Here one could make an analogy between Omar and FitzGerald. They both had an independent income, they both were indolent, and their philosophy and beliefs varied with the mood and the day, the intrinsic difference being that, though now and then in Doubting Castle, blasphemy was unknown to FitzGerald. But blasphemy to the Oriental means something quite different, and because of this the flimsy bridge between Suffolk and Persia would collapse under the weight of the analogy.

Professor Cowell, who, so to speak, brought Omar to FitzGerald, was an accomplished Persian scholar, a man of integrity and of standards which were the best symbols of his age. He has summed Omar up thus:

His terastichs are filled with bitter satires of the sensuality and hypocricy of the pretenders to sanctity, but he did not stop there. He could see with a clear eye the evil and folly of charlatans and empirics: but he was blind when he turned from these, to deny the existence of the soul's disease, or at any rate of the possibility of a cure. Here, like Lucretius, he cut himself loose from facts: and in both alike we trace the unsatisfied instincts—the dim conviction that their wisdom is folly—which reflect themselves in darker colours in the misanthropy and despair which cloud their visions of life.

FitzGerald felt differently. Of the Rubáiyát, by which after all Omar is known to us, he said to Laurence, the painter: ". . . a sort of *triste Plaisir* in it as others beside myself have felt. It is a desperate sort of thing, unfortunately at the bottom of all thinking men's minds: but made Music of."

The music was by FitzGerald, but was there true despair in Omar? Baudelaire loved the dregs of the cup; hence, he despaired of himself and the cup, too. Omar loved the cup and, since everything was in the hands of Fate, he took the cup and himself as the mood dictated.

Much play has been made of his symbolism; but, if foreigners begin at Calais, so does the vernacular realism of symbolism, and it gathers speed as it travels southeast, or rather the nearer it gets to home. When Mussolini's son, describing an air attack on Abyssinian horsemen during the Abyssinian war, spoke of the bombed horsemen opening up like red roses, in England and America those lines were quoted with horror. As a matter of fact, it was simply his vernacular, a *façon de parler*.

In the preface to the third edition of the Rubáiyát FitzGerald denies that Omar was debauched: "Other readers," he says, "may be content to believe with me that while the Wine Omar celebrates is simply the Juice of the Grape, he bragg'd more than he drank of it, in very defiance perhaps of that Spiritual Wine which left its Votaries sunk in Hypocrisy or Disgust."

But FitzGerald also believed the tale of the three friends who swore brotherhood and, as to bragging, one usually brags only of congenial matters.

The cup was the cup, and drunkenness was a good sensation. The book of verses, the jug of wine, the loaf of bread, and the lover singing were the natural desires of a man of Omar's learning, thirst, hunger, and passion. And if one drinks and loves under a hot sun, then one does wish to be laid shrouded in the living leaf by some not unfrequented garden-side; and then, needless to say, the rising moon will look for one in vain. It is all very sad: death is a sort of hangover, so one gets somewhat blasphemous and, because one knows absolutely nothing of Christian ethics, one is quite impolite to one's Maker. As one had emptied many glasses that had brimmed with wine, one's final picture of oneself, shrouded in self-pity, is an empty glass.

Omar in his own country was considered a third-rate poet. Persian poetry is fixed by conventions, meters, ordering of rhymes, the sequence of subjects, the permissible comparisons, similes, and metaphors, the varieties of rhetorical embellishments, all according to a rigid rule; judged by these rules, Omar is found lacking. Nevertheless, in the West he is still the best-known Persian poet, though that is not on his account but because of FitzGerald.

Rubáiyát is Persian for quatrains, and not all the quatrains which FitzGerald included in the Rubáiyát are ascribed to Omar. There were "wandering quatrains," as the scholar has it, but the scholar cannot definitely state which were Omar's and which were composed by others. Since they all entered FitzGerald's light and were molded by him, one can, though not irreverently, here dispense with the scholar, especially as FitzGerald himself was no Persian scholar.

His road to Omar was slow and far from straight. Perhaps if he had not met Professor Cowell—but to speculate on that is as idle and foolish as to try to picture what would have happened if Columbus had not discovered America.

Edward Byles Cowell was born in Ipswich in 1826 in a house in St. Clements Street. He went to Ipswich Grammar School. His father was a merchant and he was destined to go into his father's business. However, young Cowell preferred the study of Spanish, Italian, and Sanskrit to the intricacies of business and malting. He met FitzGerald around 1845. By then he had already translated some Persian poetry. In 1847 he married Elisabeth Charlesworth, the daughter of the Rector of Flowton. She was fourteen years older than he. They went to live in a cottage at Bramford, and there FitzGerald frequently visited them. To them, as to so many others, he gave his full friendship and love. The story goes that Fitz-Gerald had been in love with Mrs. Cowell: the story can be dismissed, as can the similar tale about Caroline Crabbe.

Mrs. Cowell was a woman of strength. She persuaded her husband to turn his back on his father's business and to go to Oxford and start on an academic career.

She was well rewarded: by 1856 he was Professor of English History at Calcutta University, and a well-known Sanskrit scholar. In 1867 he became the first Professor of Sanskrit at Cambridge.

Cowell was a man of refinement and learning, with a lovable disposition. A true friend of FitzGerald, he let FitzGerald go his way—which was far from his own—without reproach, and he was always ready to help. He worshiped his much older wife and, after her death, felt that his life had ended too; but on he went, gently, dignified. The posthumous life of the scholar is like a small candle which, apart from the few who are in need of it, nobody observes. Consequently it is good to know that his name will always be associated with that of FitzGerald, thus assuring him an immortality which he well deserves.

As far back as 1846 FitzGerald had told Cowell that it would be "a good work to give us some of the good things of Hafiz and the Persians: of bulbuls and ghouls we have had enough."

In order to write a letter or to give himself over to study, FitzGerald needed before him a kind, friendly face. With Cowell he found it and, in his lazy fashion, he persevered with Persian, the language which Cowell, as it were, had brought to his notice. He had turned to Persian because Cowell studied it; it would be pleasant to be able to discuss a subject dear to his friend's heart.

So the road to the Rubáiyát was also the road of his friendship.

In 1854 FitzGerald wrote from Geldestone Hall, Beccles:

I came here ten days ago, and have just (and only just) taken up Zuleikha. I find it hard but really very good at the beginning; and I pursue the original plan of making the German teach me Persian and Vice Versa—I think a really good plan. I had previously picked up some of the grammatical forms of German from Ollendorf and also got my nieces to read with me a little here; and I find the German thus both Assisting and Assisted.

When the Cowells left for Calcutta, FitzGerald was miserable. His friend far away on the shores of the Ganges was another reason to continue with the Persian. It was a votive offering. "As to India being 'your place' it may be; but as to you being lost in England, that could not be," wrote FitzGerald, and when he said England he thought of himself, but he thought, too, of going out to India. He had to admit he had always been slow in getting under way, and left it at that.

To the end of his life they were close friends; Cowell invariably stood up for him though Cowell knew best how unscholarly the Rubáiyát was. The much discussed 58th quatrain of the first edition FitzGerald had rendered as follows:

Oh, Thou who Man of baser Earth didst make,
And who with Eden didst devise the Snake;
For all the Sin wherewith the Face of Man
Is blackn'd, Man's Forgiveness give—and take!

The correct translation is:

Oh thou who knowest the secrets of everyone's mind
Who graspest everyone's hand in the hour of weakness
Oh God, give me repentance and accept my excuses
Oh Thou who givest repentance and acceptest the excuses
of everyone.

"FitzGerald," said Cowell, "mistook the meaning of giving and accepting as used here and so invented his last line out of his own mistake. I wrote to him about it when I was in Calcutta, but he never cared to alter it."

Probably FitzGerald thought that by misunderstanding Persian he understood Omar better.

Ten years after FitzGerald's death, Cowell summed him up for the benefit of Aldis Wright like this:

Some of his letters were most remarkable for their occasional fragments of fine criticism—little bits of the purest gold. *The Bird-Parliament* well deserves to be published. Some parts of it are really magnificent. He originally sent it to me in India to be printed in our Bengal Asiatic Sc. journal (I was the Oriental Secretary then) but I felt it was too free and unscientific to be printed in such a journal. Still it well deserves to remain with Omar Kh. & the Jamí and the Greek tragedies. They are all alike in being too free to be called translations—yet what chosen translations could ever give such vivid idea of the original? I should like exceedingly to read the two Oedipuses. It is curious that in the old days he often told Tennyson that he (Tennyson) should leave at least one of Sophocles's plays translated. Every great poet, he used to say, owes this as a duty to his predecessors.

At any rate, FitzGerald, without ever considering himself great, fulfilled that duty.

Both Jamí's *Salámán and Absál* and Attar's *Bird-Parliament* were inferior to the Rubáiyát; but *The Bird-Parliament* is a fine thing, and were it not compared with the almost overbearing excellence of the Rubáiyát, it would rank as a first-class work of art. In *The Bird-Parliament* FitzGerald caught his own mood. The plot appealed to him, it was according to his heart. He loved birds, and here the birds assemble, for a king has to be chosen. It is not easy: many have strong claims. Eventually the Tajidar, the Persian lapwing, is selected:

> *The tajidar said,*
> *One Night from the swarming City Gate*
> *Stept Holy Bajazyd to meditate*
> *Alone amid the breathing Fields that lay*
> *In solitary Silence leagues away,*
> *Beneath a Moon and Stars as bright as Day.*
> *And the Saint wondering such a Temple were,*
> *And so lit up, and scarce one worshipper,*

A voice from Heav'n amid the stillness said:
"The Royal Road is not for all to tread,
Nor is the Royal Palace for the Rout,
Who, even if they reach it, are shut out.
The Blaze that from my Harim window breaks
With fright the Rabble of the Roadside takes;
And ev'n of those that at my Portal din,
Thousands may knock for one that enters in."

So the Tajidar and a chosen flock of birds set out under his leadership; the more worldly of the birds remain behind. The select company travel till they attain the vision of God.

"Be it even so:
Let us see the Fount from which we flow,
And seeing lose Ourselves therein!" And, Lo!
Before the Word was utter'd, or the Tongue
Of Fire replied, or Portal open flung,
They were within—they were before the Throne.
Before the Majesty that sat thereon,
But wrapt in so insufferable a Blaze
Of Glory as beat down their baffled Gaze,
Which, downward dropping, fell upon a Scroll
That, Lightning-like, flash'd back on each the whole
Half-forgotten Story of his Soul:

The birds were abashed and, in full confession and self-loathing, flung away the carnal self. In the soul's integrity reclothed they lifted their eyes and in the center

of the glory they beheld themselves, and a voice of awful
Answer spoke to them, the voice of the Tajidar:

> *I was the Sin that from Myself rebell'd:*
> *I the Remorse that tow'rd Myself compell'd:*
> *I was the Tajidar who led the Track:*
> *I was the little Briar that pull'd you back:*
> *Sin and Contrition—Retribution owed,*
> *And cancell'd—Pilgrim, Pilgrimage, and Road,*
> *Was but Myself towards Myself: and Your*
> *Arrival but Myself at my own Door:*
> *Who in your Fraction of Myself behold*
> *Myself within the Mirror Myself hold*
> *To see Myself in, and each part of Me*
> *That sees himself, though drown'd, shall ever see.*
> *Come you lost Atoms in your Centre daw,*
> *And be the Eternal Mirror that you saw:*
> *Rays that have wander'd into Darkness wide*
> *Return, and back into your Sun subside.*

Truly, FitzGerald very near his best.

Nowadays the word "promise" is frequently used.
Our age seems longer in maturing, though the promise
of violent death always at our elbow should make us
hurry up. Our poets and writers are full of promise, even
after their hair turns gray or falls out altogether. Today
we examine the works of our contemporaries in the
kindly light of promise to be fulfilled at some distant

232

date; with the Victorians promise was something one had to shed much earlier. Therefore, one cannot judge *Salámán and Absál* and *The Bird-Parliament* as part of the promise which culminated in the Rubáiyát. On the other hand, one can marvel at the immense difference both in touch and vision which separates *Salámán and Absál* from the Rubáiyát; and the answer to the marvel is, again, the mystery of FitzGerald's communion with Omar.

The Bird-Parliament can well stand on its own. Fitz-Gerald, as I have said, had a high opinion of it. The idea of birds going on a pilgrimage was according to his taste; the idea of worldly birds returning to their worldly occupations and not joining in the pilgrimage appealed to him because he disliked the world; and then one reads with surprise in *Polonius:* "One sees this fault in the Eastern fables. Birds and beasts are made to *reason*, instead of representing the passions and affections they really share with men."

On second thought, that remark is not surprising. In his own works FitzGerald attached less importance to thought than to sentiment. (In *Euphranor* there is plenty of thought, which is the weakness of the book.) The quality of elation in his writing arises from his repressed senses and not from his shrewd, open-eyed, amused mind. This is true of the Rubáiyát, too. The quatrains:

With them the seed of Wisdom did I sow,
And with mine own hand wrought to make it grow;
*   And this was all the Harvest that I reap'd—*
"I came like Water, and like Wind I go."

and

We are no other than a moving row
Of Magic Shadow-shapes that come and go
*   Round with the Sun-illumined Lantern held*
In Midnight by the Master of the Show;

are, apart from the already discussed Eastern symbolism of Omar, good examples of fine form and small conviction.

It is not FitzGerald's fault that the agnostic found in the Rubáiyát his own highest expression. The Rubáiyát has suited many tastes. (I remember, in the twenties—which were, after all, not bad years—a dear lady with jade earrings and Liberty gowns explaining to me that the Rubáiyát had urged her to adultery. It would have been very unfair, had her husband blamed FitzGerald.) Agnosticism gathered speed at the turn of the century. FitzGerald had been dead nearly two decades; yet it was at the turn of the century that the Rubáiyát was acclaimed as the hymn of the unbeliever.

FitzGerald, at any rate, had not approached his task of rendering the Quatrains into English with the zeal of one who wants to give the world a new, daring doctrine.

234

Cowell had come across the Ouseley Collection in the Bodleian and had made a copy for FitzGerald.

The work of translating was not an easy task. "I am not always certain of getting the right sow by the ear," he would ruefully say. Though conscientious with the form, he was not painstaking with the exact meaning of words. In all four editions of the Rubáiyát he made changes, but they are more changes of thought and form than of meaning. He worked on it while staying with Browne in Bedfordshire, and would put down the manuscript when Browne's filly came up and sniffed about him. And there were buttercups and a delicious breeze.

In 1857 Cowell sent him a copy of the Calcutta manuscript. Edward Heron-Allen, who devoted unlimited time to the study of the Rubáiyát, stated that forty-nine of the quatrains were from the Ouseley manuscript, or the Calcutta manuscript, or both. Forty-four were traceable to more than one quatrain and were, therefore, composite quatrains. Two were found by FitzGerald only in J. R. Nicolas's text; two reflected the whole spirit of the original poem; two were traceable to the influence of *The Mantik ut-tair* of Perid ud din Attár; and two quatrains, primarily inspired by Omar, were influenced by *The Odes* of Hafiz.

In the spring of 1857 Fitzgerald wrote to Garcin de Tassy, a Persian scholar in Paris. Later he sent him a copy of the Rubáiyát, and Garcin de Tassy wrote a

235

paper on it for the *Journal Asiatique*, to which FitzGerald's reaction was that England instead of France should have ingratiated herself first with Persia. That he meant as a joke, for the thought that he, the lazy inaccurate translator, could do anything for England, or France, in Persia must have made him laugh. FitzGerald's ambitions were deep down and, as with his other feelings, afraid of light.

Lazy or not lazy, he fought hard with the Rubáiyát. ". . . anything," he wrote to Cowell, "like a literal Translation would be, I think, unreadable; and what I have done for amusement is not only so unliteral, but I doubt unoriental, in its form and expression, as would destroy the value of the Original without replacing it with anything worth reading of my own. It has amused me however to reduce the Mass into something of an Artistic Shape."

Another conscious daytime reaction made him tell Cowell that Omar's philosophy was one that never failed in the world. "Today is ours, etc." But the day, at the time, was not FitzGerald's, for he was living in lodgings in London with his wife Lucy. So only yesterday was his; but that, too, suited Omar's mood.

I like, indeed, A. C. Benson's simile about the Rubáiyát. It has, he said, received from its admirers the sort of treatment, the poking and pushing, conceded to prize animals at shows; I should never dare to become one of the pokers and pushers. Heron-Allen pushed and poked for nearly a lifetime. I, for one, preferred to sit on FitzGerald's grave and listen to the utter silence of the Boulge summer evening, with two rabbits in my shooting bag, and the distant sound of a tractor unable to disturb the silence—in fact, it intensified it.

However, Heron-Allen did excellent work, and I take at random two quatrains with the literal translation of Heron-Allen and with FitzGerald's rendering of them. FitzGerald's quatrain:

> For some we loved, the loveliest and the best
> That from his Vintage rolling Time hath prest,
>   Have drunk their Cup a Round or two before,
> And one by one crept silently to rest.

Persian text as translated by Heron-Allen:

> All my sympathetic friends have left me,
> One by one they have sunk low at the foot of Death.
> In the fellowship of souls they were cup-companions,
> A turn or two before me they became drunk.

FitzGerald's quatrain:

> Why, be this Juice the growth of God, who dare
> Blaspheme the twisted tendril as a Snare?
>   A Blessing we should use it, should we not?
> And if a Curse—Why, then, Who set it there?

Persian text as translated by Heron-Allen:

I drink wine, and everyone drinks who, like me, is worthy
  of it;
My wine-drinking is but a small thing to Him;
God knew on the Day of Creation that I should drink wine;
If I do not drink wine God's knowledge would be ignorance.

These two examples should be enough food for endless thought, but such thought, after a time, becomes a
vicious circle. Besides, the beauty of an old room consists
partly of now and then getting out of it in order to think
pleasurably of it out in the light. And so it is with the
four editions of the Rubáiyát. FitzGerald polished, left
out, put back, chopped and changed with every new
edition. One could analyze each edition (it has often
been done) and reach any conclusion one wished. In
one's enthusiasm one might quite forget that Fitz-
Gerald, with much time on his hands, with his keen
sense of words and form, might simply have made the
changes because he thought he could improve the
whole. The work would also make time fly while he
waited for Posh, or when he was too bored to go down
to the Deben or take a walk.

In 1858 FitzGerald sent the manuscript of the Rubáiyát to *Frazer's Magazine.* A year went by and nothing
happened. He took the manuscript back and published
it himself—a small quarto, in a brown paper wrapper,
which I have reverently handled in Trinity Library,

Cambridge. Two hundred and fifty copies were printed; a few he gave to his friends, the rest he sent to Bernard Quaritch, and there they languished for nearly two years, until Quaritch dumped them into his bargain box to be discovered by two friends of Rossetti, Messrs. Witley Stokes and Ormsby. Each bought a copy for one penny. And here Swinburne comes in. Though personally unknown to each other, he and FitzGerald had a friend in common, Richard Monkton Milnes, first Lord Houghton, the quondam Cambridge Apostle, on whose shoulder not only Rogers' breakfast mantle had fallen, but who was also the owner of a robust pornographic library in which Swinburne spent more time than was perhaps good for him.

Having read the Rubáiyát, Swinburne wrote:

Rossetti and I invested upwards of sixpence apiece—or possibly threepence—I would not wish to exaggerate our extravagance—in copies at that not exorbitant price. Next day we thought we might get some more for presents among our friends, but the man at the stall asked twopence! Rossetti expostulated with him in terms of such humourously indignant remonstrance as none but he could ever have commanded. We took a few and left him. In a week or two, if I am not much mistaken, the remaining copies were sold at a guinea. . . .

"But at all Cost," FitzGerald had told Cowell of the Rubáiyát, "a Thing must *live*"; and now it had begun.

239

FitzGerald, afraid of his own ambition, pretending to have none, was not an easy person for a publisher to deal with. Quaritch had not an easy time with him. If one pretends not to be moved by applause, one becomes easily a prima donna; and FitzGerald behaved like one to Quaritch. Though he was in no need of money, he complained to Aldis Wright that Quaritch was too keen a businessman, and called him by not flattering epithets. Yet all Quaritch wanted was more editions of the Rubáiyát, as one of his letters, dated November 18, 1878, shows:

Dear Sir

Do let me reprint the Rubáiyát!

I have so many enquiries for copies that it is painful to be unable to supply a want felt by that part of the public with which I desire to be in connection and which you as the poet idolized by a small but choice circle, ought to be anxious to gratify personally, rather than throw into the hands of American pirates the opportunity of reprinting and misprinting *ad libidum*.

Allow me to publish another edition and pay you twenty-five guineas as the honorarium. You know it would be well done and creditable to us both.

Perhaps it was Quaritch's gushing style or the prima donna's reluctance to play, but FitzGerald continued to refer unfavorably to Quaritch. When Aldis Wright suggested to Quaritch that the Rubáiyát should not be reprinted with romans and italics, Quaritch replied that

he could not take his advice because italics between romans were a pleasant relief, keeping the reader's attention from flagging. "It was Cowley, I think," added
Quaritch, "who had said: 'Tell her such differing chords
make all our harmony.' "

From that not too tactful letter it is conceivable that
it was more the man than the publisher whom FitzGerald disliked. Nevertheless, Quaritch continued to publish and FitzGerald to grumble, which is, more or less,
the usual relationship which exists between publisher
and author.

Ruskin was among the early admirers. On September
2, 1853, he wrote:

My dear and very dear Sir,

I do not know in the least who you are, but I do with all
my soul pray you to find and translate some more of Omar
Khayyám for us. I never did till this day read anything so
glorious to my mind as this poem (10th, 11th, 12th pages
if you were to choose)—and this and this is all I can say
about it. More—more—please more—and that I am ever
                    Gratefully and respectfully yours,
                                            J. Ruskin

The pages Ruskin referred to contained Quatrains
XLV to LVIII.

What FitzGerald thought of such a letter and of the
enthusiasm of the few worshipers is difficult to tell, difficult chiefly because he had, in some respects, the sly-

ness and simplicity of the countryman. His life had been lived mostly either deep in the country or in the provincial town of Woodbridge, with the fields running, in his day, almost to Market Hill. In Thackeray's time he had begun to turn his back on the metropolitan world; after a while he not only renounced this world but feared it, too. It is possible that his modesty about the Rubáiyát was inspired by that fear. Londoners were coming into the country; surely they had some hidden, cunning reason for it: one had better beware.

If one lives most of one's life among pollard oaks and church steeples, one becomes a little like them; and church steeples and oaks do not willingly give their shadows to strangers.

There is one more matter of interest concerning the relationship between FitzGerald and Omar. It has often been asked why he had chosen Jamí, Attar, and Omar, and not a giant like Firdausi. Up to a point, it is again Professor Cowell who supplies the answer.

He had always [wrote Cowell a month after FitzGerald's death] felt a keen interest in Firdausi's sympathy with the Pre-Mohammedan history and religion, though he never cared much for the *Shahmamah* itself as poetry. He never cared for that kind of ballad epic—I could never get him to read the poem of Cid in Spanish. FitzGerald sympathised with Firdausi's interest in the old fire-worship—the Magian fire temple of the forgotten 2nd Avesta, but he soon tired of the long episodes and endless wars in the old poem itself. He often said he never cared much about the *Iliad* or its heroes.

The subject of FitzGerald's relationship with Omar and the Rubáiyát is almost inexhaustible; but one wonders whether the Rubáiyát itself will not exhaust, in due course, its worshipers and public. It is, I believe, less read today than it was twenty years ago. Too many people have quoted it for their own purposes, and too many ribbons of too many colors have been attached to it. It might, at some not quite distant date, find a temporary obscurity. The trend today is toward Christianity, the stand-by of troubled ages, and nowadays, having so proudly strayed from it, man finds himself in a pretty deep morass. The cross in a Scottish mist will become preferable to the sun on the Ganges. When that day comes, the Rubáiyát, not because of FitzGerald but because of his enthusiasts, will be less read—perhaps not read at all.

It is a sad thought that the man who played the organ in churches and chapels, whose daily life exuded Christian charity, should have to enter temporary oblivion because of the interpretation others put on his work. But that obscurity could not become complete, for there still remain his letters, which are among the best in the language. They are delightful, mostly beautifully written, and full of an intangible yet penetrating joy. The letters should be read under a shady tree in summer, in the evening as a preparation for pleasant dreams, on top of buses in order to forget the noise of the street—in short, anywhere one is in need of a good, gay companion.

FitzGerald, had fate and Mary Frances forced him into an occupation, probably would have made his name as a critic. He would have been a somewhat crotchety critic, prone to praise the dead and ready to condemn the living. He would have been swayed by his emotions and his love of simplicity, which is of the country but not of the town. Even when he admitted that what he praised was no good, he still praised it if he liked it. He was devoted to his own tears.

He wrote to Fanny Kemble in November 1875:

. . . your mention of your American isolation reminds me of some Verses of Hood, with which I will break your Heart a little. They are not so very good neither: but I, in England, as I am, and like to be, cannot forget them.

> *The Swallow with Summer*
> *Shall wing o'er the Seas;*
> *The Wind that I sigh to*
> *Shall sing in your Trees;*
> *The Ship that it hastens*
> *Your Port will contain—*
> *But for me—I shall never*
> *See England again.*

It always runs through my head to a little German Air, common enough in our younger days—which I will make a note of, and you will, I dare say, remember at once.

It is doubtful whether Fanny Kemble was moved by the verses though she was far from England; but Fitz-Gerald in England was moved by them. They appealed to his heart, his tears; he had seen swallows winging like that over the pond at Boulge, and England was so beautiful that, even in England, he could long for her as if from the distance. The very idea of distance made England lovelier; but all that had little to do with the actual merit of the verses.

To be a good letter writer one must have wit. With wit FitzGerald was well endowed. One should also be something of a descriptive writer, and FitzGerald was a descriptive writer of the first order. When biographers and admirers quote the last paragraph of *Euphranor,* they do so because it is a fine piece of descriptive prose. *Polonius,* like *Euphranor,* does not make easy reading. It is jerky, yet when the reader reaches the following passage, he feels as though a boat which had been pushed along in a shallow river bed had suddenly met the deep current:

I had started one fine October morning on a ramble through the villages that lie beside the Ouse. In high health and cloudless spirits, one regret perhaps hanging upon the horizon of the heart, I walked through Sharnbrook up the hill, and paused by the church on the summit to look about me. The sun shone, the clouds flew, the yellow trees shook in the wind, the river rippled in breadths of light and dark; rooks and daws wheeled and cawed aloft in changing spaces of blue above the spire; the churchyard all still in the sunshine below.

The land, the clouds, the sea, and the trees were fine pictures which he laid, as it were, on his friends' breakfast plate. A keen observer of detail, he could reproduce for them men's thoughts, extravagancies, remarks, and doings. A joke he liked above all. When his friend Biddell married, he at once remembered the story of the clergyman who, after quoting the Bible on righteousness and peace meeting and kissing one another, concluded with these words: "Which that we may all do may God in his infinite mercy grant thee."

Sadness has its own place in his letters, but it does not take up much room; there is a fundamental undercurrent of happiness. His senses longed for the burning images of Persia, but his body and soul were well content with Suffolk; and with Suffolk and through Suffolk comes the serenity of his letters. Besides, the distance between writer and recipient was something he appreciated. It has been said that he wrote good letters because he knew he had the gift to write good letters. To say that is as silly as to reproach a good singer for singing off the concert platform now and then for friends. It is also said that he modeled himself on Madame de Sévigné whose letters he often reread. That does not hold good. He read her letters because he liked her. He and Omar, if they had met, would not have got on, but had he met Madame de Sévigné and had she been able to pierce his shyness, they would have become fast friends.

He was often alone and that was one more reason to write. There is a fine rhythm that goes through the letters. I take at haphazard the ending of one: "My Ship is fitting out; the Lugger has sent me a dozen Mackerel: and I am yours always. E. FG."

The letters have come to us via Aldis Wright. I sat with the lion's share of the letters in Trinity Library, and I believed, without being able to give or find the slightest proof, that Wright must have destroyed some of them. Now and then FitzGerald could become ribald; such letters should not be edited by the future Vice Master of Trinity. I looked at Wright's portrait, which was the portrait of a hard, righteous man, a man who sat on a virtuous throne of his own making. Yet he had been FitzGerald's friend, and FitzGerald could not abide the cold and the hard. Moreover, the letters addressed to Wright were full of gaiety and the easy approach of the friend. Wright's face, therefore I concluded, was but the façade of his time, a façade that had come down to our generation without the explanation of the impulses, pretexts, and necessities his time had demanded from him.

When Wright set about editing the letters, he did it, so to speak, behind his own portrait. Unwittingly, he almost harmed FitzGerald. Once a letter writer is presented as a conscious writer of fine letters, half the charm is gone. I will furnish an example. In the *Letters of Edward FitzGerald,* Wright quotes the following, which has been quoted *ad nauseam* by admirers, biographers, in short, by anybody who wrote about Fitz-Gerald!

I run over to Lowestoft occasionally for a few days but do not abide there long: no longer having my dear little Ship for company. I saw her looking very smart under her new owner ten days ago, and I felt so at home when I was once more on her Deck that— Well I content myself with sailing on the river Deben, looking at the crops as they grow green, yellow, russet, and are finally carried away on the red and blue waggon with the sorrel horse.

The bit about green, yellow, and russet crops and the "blue waggon with the sorrel horse," quoted and quoted again as an example of FitzGerald's gift as a letter writer, makes one suspicious: the man had worked that sentence out carefully, took days over it in order to make it sound beautiful; in short, he did not write spontaneously but lingered over his letters as though he were writing an essay. He was writing for effect and posterity, but not precisely to his friends.

Now if only Wright had given the letter in its complete text, then no such suspicions would have arisen. As a proof of FitzGerald's spontaneous genius as a letter writer, I quote the whole. Perhaps the joke at the end made Wright reticent. You do not tell such jokes to a hard portrait.

Woodbridge, September 4/71.

My dear Wright?

Or are you flown from Cambridge, like all the World, for your Holiday elsewhere? Cowell wrote me that he was sure to be at Lowestoft by the middle of August: and soon after that his wife writes to my Niece that he has overdone himself, & fled to some Uncle's in Devonshire—& whither I have just written to ask about him. As Elisabeth [the wife] was not with him when she wrote, I conclude that he was not *very* much amiss, and, were he or not, I think Devonshire a better place for him than Lowestoft: more of a Change, to a far further Country, with a bluer sea, & with more Vegetation ashore to engage his botanical faculties, which (as he last wrote me) had sprung into sudden Activity. This new Study will be good if it takes him from his other Studies abroad: but not if he has to work *double-tides* indoors to make up for his rambles in the Field. If you can tell me anything of him and his health, you will oblige me: for I have told him not to answer my letter if he finds any inconvenience in so doing.

249

And you yourself—what are you doing & where sojourning? Let me know if you come Suffolkwards. I run over to Lowestoft occasionally for a few days but do not abide there long: no longer having my dear little Ship for company. I saw her there looking very smart under her new owner ten days ago, & I felt so at home when I was once more on her Deck that— Well I content myself with sailing on the river Deben, looking at the crops as they grow green, yellow, russet, and are finally carried away on the red and blue waggon with the sorrel horse.

Do you know if Horner Tookes' Etym. of "Luck" holds? AS. *loeccean,* to seize, catch etc. whence the Fisherman's "Luck." I saw this quoted in some stray Paper: & I see that Richardson approves.

Don't forget my *Carlyle Letters* etc. when you come "down East"—& believe me yours

E. FG.

An old Suffolk Farmer calling his Housekeeper to account (before a friend of mine) for not being up to make breakfast at 4½, "If'd had a Man abed with you there'd a been some excuse— But you h'ant, ha' ye?"

I think this letter proves that FitzGerald's letters were spontaneous, with no desire to create an effect, nor were they artificial: fine sentences came straight, unplanned, unmeditated. I am sure Wright laughed over the story of the farmer and housekeeper, but that was between him and FitzGerald, and not for us who can, unasked, examine his portrait. FitzGerald supplied him with another Suffolk joke, which again Wright thought better to keep to himself. That letter Wright altogether omitted to publish. The letter is dated July 27, 1877.

My dear Wright,

Here I am & shall be very happy to see you if you care to come so far to see me. I can't propose *Bed* (unless at the Inn) inasmuch as I have now four Nieces filling every cranny of my house except the room I occupy: but I can give you a bit of their 1 pm. Dinner, whether along with them or along with me, as you may prefer. So entirely please yourself.

I wish you had proposed to visit me while I was at *Dunwich* from where I only returned two days ago: putting up at a good Inn which is to be filled with other Company on Monday next— Dunwich is the prettiest place on our coast, I think: with the Walls of its old Priory of Grey Friars & some Remains of the Priory itself within them—very pathetic. If Lowell of America *should* come down here, as he thought he might, *on his way to Spain,* I would fain have asked him there: but I must say (as I said to him) that a Day's visit out of two whole Lives was scarce worth *his* troubles, & he may find enough to do in London to keep him there till he sails for his present Destination. As he is just now very warm on Cervantes his Mission is well timed, & I shall expect a good Result. For, I think he is the best of our Critics now, & that he should & could supply much that St. Beuve has left untouched. I will not ask about your White Mary, but do not suppose we shall find here what you have as yet failed to find. Had we been at Dunwich you would have found my friend Edwards there very much interested in all Suffolk topics. He was telling me as I came away of a Farmer (at Soham I think) who nicknamed his three Daughters, "Muck," "Sweat," and "Cartgrease"—not much coarser than Louis XVth's names for "Mesdemoiselles de France."

And so—Farewell—

E. FG.

You will have to drink *Sherry* now for a while? Spedding says Dr. Abbott's last Book is the *"silliest"* he ever read: & that he (J.S.) is "considering" what is to be done with it. Dreadful Rodin Pickle for the Doctor!

P.S. Two Nieces I find, leave me on *Monday* & the remaining twain on Wednesday."

Here one could mention, practically between brackets since it is of no importance, that FitzGerald's use of capitals was partly a fashion of his time and chiefly a caprice which he often quite forgot.

Undoubtedly his letters were not exercises in studied fine writing. Everything came spontaneously, and it was his letter writer's gift, coupled with the instinctive choice of the right word and rhythm, which made the sentences and thoughts flow along entwined. An acquaintance of mine, who prided himself with some justice on being a lady killer, declared that women loved him because he loved women; so FitzGerald's letters are full of life because he loved it. He did not think that the world was progressing satisfactorily; he did not share the faith of his age in machine and science; he could often despair of England; but there always remained something that could interest him, appeal to his sense of beauty and sense of the ridiculous, and nature, too, was a special friend of his. His crotchets, idiosyncrasies, and shrewd common sense, the peasant's common sense, were also with him in his letters. In the postscript of a letter to Wright he said (no date, as is frequently the case):

. . . Look into *Athenaeum* August 17th for a Notice of some conscientious Donkey who wrote a Book on *"Speech-Craft"* in order to make us all revert to pure Saxon. By the way I wd go so far (I know not if with him) as to call what I am now writing an *"Afterwrit"* simply because smoother than the clumsy *"Post script,"* though I don't want *"Forword"* for *"Preface."* Get the best out of all languages possible.

His interest in afterscript would give place to men, flowers, books, pictures: in short, anything that came within his orbit. In 1840 he wrote to his friend Thompson:

. . . A sort of Devil-may-care man in these parts who does not set up for a wit, enunciated the following theorem the other day: & as he talks very little, & deals still less in general rules, it is worthy of attention. "Everything that is, is— nothing is right—& main force is the ticket" —I laughed very much when he gave it out. He is grave in his manner & seemed convinced of his proposition.

That old cut-away Spedding—the interior of Africa—& old Alfred [Tennyson] living for a fortnight at a madhouse.

He did not want this to finish his education, I think. I went yesterday to see a Clergyman near here who cultivates about 15,000 Dahlias—each with a little pole by its side, with a little flower pot reversed on the top, to catch earwigs in— He empties these earwig pots of their content, every morning. As you may imagine, he is not dangerous.

He goes on to tell Thompson that he had visited Lord Bute's place, Luton Park, where he saw the collection of pictures—Tintoretto, Velasquez, Poussin, and a Rafael—insured for fifteen thousand pounds, but FitzGerald thought he would not give even fifteen thousand shillings for it.

From a silly man's theorem, to Alfred Tennyson, then to Old Masters through a border of dahlias, his pen moved to amuse a friend and keep in touch with him. He gave much of himself in his letters—probably more than we know; but the trouble for posterity is that letters which are perhaps too intimate and frank are often destroyed before posterity can have a say. Thus, frequently, only part of a portrait emerges, the part which the surviving contemporary considered the fittest to leave to those who would come after and, therefore, would judge. In FitzGerald's case the same effort had been made; his personality, however, was too strong to be twisted or clad in different garments than the garments he wore.

There are before me a certain number of unpublished

letters, almost all of them well worth quoting; and lief would I quote them were the old room not bidding me to move on. For that reason, let two short extracts suffice. The first is from a letter he wrote to Blanche, Donne's daughter; the second from a letter to Aldis Wright.

I have [wrote FitzGerald to Blanche Donne] been no further all this Summer than Dunwich first and then Lowestoft, which has grown large, ugly & ill-savoured from insufficient Drainage. Now I am back here again, to my old desk by day, & my young Reader of a night; we read All Year Round; *Chambers Miscellany;* Artemus Ward; & am looking forward to *Bride of Lammermoor, Pirate* & *Old Mortality* as winter deepens.

One derives obvious pleasure from that short passage and cannot help repeating: "my old desk by day, & my young Reader of a night." The second passage is of quite a personal nature.

I declare that no more Proofs should be sent to me, seeing how I dirty them. More than once with hands soiled from weeding, hoe-ing etc. & now (worse) from a bit of (I suppose) buttered Bread for Ducks etc. in the pocket where I stowed Proofs to be read "al fresco." Damn! but I'll do so no more.

If one wishes to generalize, one may say that his letters to Barton were mostly on pictures; to Frederic Tennyson on music; to Cowell on Persian, Spanish, and Greek; to Pollock and Donne on literature. He had many other correspondents, too, yet it seems to me that his best letters were those he wrote to Frederic Tennyson and to Fanny Kemble. Curiously enough, among his correspondents, they were the two of whom he saw the least. His love of the past beat through the letters, as if he had taken today and deposited it with loving hands into the past in which, for him, his two dear friends dwelt.

Part Six

POSH AND OLD AGE

O NE'S life is like a row of bells. The bell furthest
away is the bell of childhood, and when it rings it gives
out a low, distant sound; the nearest bell is the loudest,
notwithstanding it is the last bell. Therefore, when one
thinks of the dead, the hearse is more conspicuous than
the cradle. The last years appear to have more reality
than the flash of youth. In Woodbridge and around
Boulge, those who remember FitzGerald recall him as
he was when they themselves were children and he already an aged man, so naturally they think and speak
of him only as the old, stooping, baldheaded eccentric
of whom they stood in awe. FitzGerald, as if to please
them, had at any rate aged early.

In a provincial town like Woodbridge it is not easy
to go unnoticed. For a man like FitzGerald to walk down
Church Street was, from the townsfolks' point, a daily

sensation. The legends grew and there was plenty of food for them.

The FitzGerald family was conspicuous, indeed. To begin with, they were not Suffolk people. True, Mr. Edward and his brothers and sister had been born in Suffolk, but the parents were foreigners. But they had been rich: Suffolk is not impervious to money. They had lived in great style: gold plate, four-in-hand, and the rest of the bag of tricks of the rich. Then the father had gone bankrupt, the mother had left him, and there at Boulge Hall was Mr. John, who, though every room was full of clocks and Old Nelly chiming over the stable, rang for his valet when he wished to know what the time was. Mr. John's curious behavior in church and chapel made tongues wag, too. Mr. Edward had left Miss Barton shortly after their marriage. The FitzGeralds were a rum lot, a mad lot, and even Mr. Edward had admitted that they were mad, all of them—but he at least knew that he was mad.

One laughed over or sneered at the family eccentricities, but where Lucy was concerned, Woodbridge had a grudge: FitzGerald had married "step-a-yard" and then had deserted her. They could call Lucy "step-a-yard" but she was still Lucy Barton of Woodbridge, whose father had been the Woodbridge poet of whom Woodbridge was proud. Moreover, she had been one of them: the daughter of a burgher. FitzGerald was of the gentry and, by leaving the bank clerk's daughter, had shown that his class had not yet given up despising the order to which clerks, auctioneers, and corn merchants belonged. Not a nice person to know, and the company he kept was not the sort of company one would expect a gentleman of means to keep. And there was the matter of the company he did not keep. It was that company which so much disliked him. And let it be admitted that FitzGerald had become an extremely rude man. To be consistently rude is at times rather exhausting, yet he succeeded, without undue effort, in being rude to strangers most of the time.

One can grope for several explanations. He had loved vehemently, but only with heart and mind. He had not given up the world completely, nor was he insensitive to it, so his virgin life must have weighed on him. Unfulfilled appetites are allied with irascibility, and irascibility is the bedfellow of rudeness. According to pigeonhole fanciers, FitzGerald, the letter writer and translator, had little imagination. That I disbelieve, but there was a certain lack of imagination when new faces appeared in his tight life. He did not like them. The idea of meeting somebody new, of having occasion to appraise a new line of thought, meant little or nothing to him. Also he feared new ties and was generally afraid of people approaching him, notwithstanding the fact that to the last he made new friends, such as Edwards the painter, and Keane of *Punch*.

Then, too, because he could not confess to himself that he was ambitious, he did not admit that his literary career had not brought the fruits which, in their own triumphs, Thackeray and Tennyson had found so delicious. One likes to stand apart as long as the door is a little ajar; nobody, for one reason or another, came through his. After a while, he simply banged the door.

He not only disliked new faces; he disliked new books, too, and aptly combined his rudenesses, in a way which is still remembered, in his behavior to a bookseller. The bookseller in question was a Mr. Reid of Ipswich. FitzGerald went to his shop, bought Wesley's *Journal,* and one day sent Mr. Reid a message asking him to dinner the following Sunday. By then FitzGerald was living in his third and last Woodbridge residence: Little Grange. Mr. Reid drove to the house, rang the bell. The housekeeper appeared and Mr. Reid told her that Mr. FitzGerald was expecting him to dinner. The housekeeper said Mr. Reid could not see the master. In vain the bookseller remonstrated, in vain he showed her the invitation: Mr. FitzGerald would not see him that day. Deeply hurt, the bookseller left. Next day he had a note from FitzGerald, saying: "I saw you yesterday when you called, but I was not fit for company, and felt I could not be bothered." That, one feels, did not alleviate the bookseller's pain.

There is no excuse for such rudeness, and FitzGerald was not interested in excuses. The pebble one throws into the pond makes, as has been too often pointed out, larger and larger ripples. When he and Thackeray parted after their trip to Paris, FitzGerald decided to become a great bear, and he truly was one, in the latter part of his life. The children of Woodbridge were frightened of him. The children, who are now very old people, told me so themselves.

Here again is an opportunity to listen to the two strangers of the Ipswich Public Library:

Query: Was E.FG. vegetarian in strict sense?

Answer: Not entirely; he would eat a little fish, game or fowl occasionally.

Query: If so who were his ducks (in pond) for?

Answer: He might give a pair away but I don't remember him eating his own fowls.

Query: Sense of humor?

Answer: He had a great sense of humor. Edward laughed quietly.

Query: Good conversationalist?

Answer: I should say so.

Query: Did you ever hear him play on an organ he

had upstairs at Little Grange? He had also a piano downstairs. He was very fond of music.

Answer: I don't remember him playing a piano but should say that he was no mean performer on the organ and sometimes accompanied it very sweetly with his voice.

Query: Did he visit with you?

Answer: When he spent an evening with me and my wife he generally came about 8 o'clock—talked of his books, old friends, people he had known and known of. Never of the day. Pictures, birds, flowers etc. Enjoyed a Welsh rarebit, pudding, macaroni or fruit at 9 o'clock supper. He generally smoked a new pipe after supper. Was fond of the old "Churchwarden"—had a glass of gin and water, occasionally another half glass and left at 11 o'clock. Whatever *he* thought of Sunday he kept it quietly and wished others to have their day of rest. Having a *thorough contempt* for the fashionable parson of the present day—he had close friends among the Highest, most learned and most Godly clergy of his time.

Query: What kind of desk in sitting room?

Answer: A desk on high legs with a drawer under the sloping top for writing on. Always stood at it.

Query: Daily habits? Time of getting up etc.

Answer: Generally fairly early and when fine walked in his garden or on his "Quarter Deck" backwards and forwards before breakfast. Dinner at noon (1 o'clock generally).

Query: Working hours?

Answer: Generally from breakfast to dinner.

Query: Reading hours?

Answer: Afternoon when wet or morning when not writing—having his reading boy at night.

The legend of the eccentric garrulous old man grew. If one is rude to you and takes little notice of you, then you must find an excuse to placate your pride. Therefore FitzGerald was declared to be mad; it was as good an excuse as any. Thus, when he took sail to Holland to see Paul Potter's "Bull," the story was spread that having reached the mouth of the Maas, he found a favorable homeward wind and sailed back. Actually he did stay two days in Holland, but that, of course, would spoil the story. According to Francis Hindes Groome, Archdeacon Groome's son, the story must have been invented by FitzGerald himself. That is quite probable, since the only bull the burghers of Woodbridge have ever heard of is the Bull Hotel in Market Place.

The story, invented or not by FitzGerald, persisted, and to that story was added another: on his way to Scotland he saw at Newcastle, from his compartment window, a train ready to leave for London, so he changed to the London train. Such stories are amusing to a point;

they aid the FitzGerald legend but have little to do with FitzGerald himself. His madness, if any, was under his own control, and eccentricity is, after all, nothing else but not conforming with the masses' ideas of proper thought and deportment.

Though rude when he felt like it, a lace-like gentleness of soul was always with him. Once Archdeacon Groome, who was a collector of Suffolk folklore, sent him a Suffolk story entitled "The Only Darter." FitzGerald was deeply moved by it and sent it on to Wright with these words: "I send you Groome's 'Only Darter' which I think so good that I shall get him to let me print it for others beside those of the Ips. *Journal*. It seems to me a beautiful Suffolk 'Idyll.' (Why not Eidyll?)"

He had many copies printed which he gave away to his friends. He often talked of it; and the story, a good sad tale, is chiefly interesting because he found his own feelings mirrored in it. In a lopsided fashion it is the story of FitzGerald's own heart.

"The Only Darter" is written in Suffolk dialect. It is the story of a poor Suffolk girl as related by her father. She did not get on with her stepmother, so she traveled to London where she went into service in a lodging house. Susan, the only daughter, had to run upstairs the whole day long. There was an old gentleman who "one daa he rung three times, but Susan was set fast and coon't go; and when she did he spook so sharp, that it wholly upset her and she dropt down o' the floor all in a faint." She was taken to a hospital. She was "breedin' a faver." In the hospital they were kind to her, the doctor came round to see her every day.

The happy climax of her stay came when a young gentleman in the company of other young gentlemen, namely medical students, came with an oddish gentleman to her bedside and, having heard her broad Suffolk accent, said to her: "Do yeou cum out o' Suffolk?"

Delighted, Susan replied: "Yes; what, do yeou know me?"

After a while she got better and the doctor sent her home. The father went to meet her at Halesworth but her appearance was not satisfactory. "O lawk, a lawk!" he exclaimed. "How bad she did look." He took her home and his wife had a good fire ready for her and ivrything nice for her but the poor mor (girl) was wholly beat. The stepmother looked after her; however, poor Susan was sinking. She was grateful to her stepmother, in fact one day she kissed her and said: "Kiss me mother dear, yeou're a good mother to me." Her father overheard that and it made him werry comfortable. The end soon came. It was at night and she had just sung a hymn. Never had she sung so sweetsome before. Father and stepmother went to her side. She was as white as sheets.

Stepmother said, "Yeou're a dyin' dear."

"Well then," said Susan, " 'tis bewtiful."

She looked hard at both of them and then lookt up smilin' as if she see Some One.

"She was," the father ends the story, "the only darter I ivver had."

The simplicity, the pathos, the lack of cant of the tale were all FitzGerald's and he must have wished in the Christian charity of his soul to have been with Susan at the hospital where he would have given her good things to eat (even some of his ducks) and plenty of gay flowers. He would have loved to accompany the sweetsome hymn on the organ and then to have rewarded father and stepmother. It seemed to me when I read "The Only Darter" that it was a bright warm light which lit up the old room into which I had wandered; and in that light I completely forgot the bookseller called Mr. Reid and the frightened Woodbridge children.

His long pilgrimage through Woodbridge had three stations: Farlingay Hall, his lodgings in Market Hill, and Little Grange. He was at Farlingay Hall when Carlyle came to stay with him. His friendship with Carlyle was the sign of his tolerance. They had practically nothing in common. Though often despairing of life, FitzGerald still loved it; Carlyle despised it. FitzGerald lacked pomposity; Carlyle was never without it. Fitz-Gerald loved liberty; Carlyle abhorred it. Even his dog was for Carlyle a "poor little animal, so loyal, so loving, so naïve and true, with what of dim intellect he had." Yet as it happens to lovers of the superman, Carlyle was nevertheless flattered when the owner of the dim intellect jumped about in front of him on its hind legs.

A certain evening in London, having for a longish while listened to Carlyle, FitzGerald, as he left, heard the sounds of a hurdy-gurdy playing a waltz, and since it was a cheerful change from the Sage he waltzed off into the night. Carlyle, one supposes, shook his head disapprovingly and returned to his dreams of heavy Prussian boots and the downfall of the French.

But friends they were and friends they remained, though one has the impression that most of the friendship was of FitzGerald's making. So it was with the majority of his friendships.

Before Carlyle came to stay with him in the summer of 1862, FitzGerald wrote to him: "I will do my best to entertain you, by giving you what food you will *at the inn* close to my lodgings: taking you to Sea in my little Ship—and—leaving you alone."

In the same letter FitzGerald, who would do anything for his friend except pretend to think and feel that which he did not, said: "You won't care a bit, I am sure, when I—(or perhaps any one else) tell you I don't care so much for Frederic! Perhaps you don't yourself . . . don't say this to show off any impertinent frankness."

On August 8 Carlyle arrived. Jane Carlyle had already explained to FitzGerald her husband's needs and wants. Carlyle arrived with many books, making it clear at once that he needed hours of solitude every day. They were given, and FitzGerald was like an attentive chamberlain to him. When Carlyle was in the right mood he was taken to Aldborough or Dunwich or Framlingham; if he was prepared for company, he was driven to Bredfield to meet the Crabbes; and if it was rustic quiet he wanted, he got it with FitzGerald sitting at his feet under a tree. FitzGerald did his best; nonetheless one serious mishap occurred. On the second night of the monumental visit a lot of rude cattle came under the Sage's window and with their lowing interrupted his sleep. Because of that, notwithstanding FitzGerald's renewed offers of hospitality, the visit was not repeated.

Carlyle and FitzGerald continued to meet now and then. FitzGerald nursed his love, but mostly in his heart; Carlyle's heaviness and readiness to be the dark cloud before the sun were probably too much for him. Even Carlyle's letters, which were usually long-delayed answers to the friendly cheerful ones FitzGerald wrote, were pretty joyless. "I," wrote Carlyle in November

1874, "lingered in Scotland latterly against my will, for almost six weeks: the scenes there never can cease to be impressive to me, indeed as natural in late visits they are far more impressive, and I have to wander there like a solitary ghost among the graves of those that are gone from me, sad, sad, I always think while there, ought not this visit be the last?"

After FitzGerald had visited Edinburgh and Abbotsford, he received an equally uncheerful letter: "By all means go again to Edinburgh. (Tho' the old city is so shorn of its old grim beauty & is become a place of Highland shawls & railway shrieks) . . ."

Before Carlyle's eightieth birthday, in 1875, a subscription for a gold medal with Carlyle's likeness was set up to commemorate it. FitzGerald did not feel like subscribing to it. Gold medals held not his sympathy. Eventually he did subscribe, but considered the whole thing of address, medal, and white scroll rather a cockney affair; and he was certain that a few years before, Carlyle would have blown his nose upon it; but, he added, he never saw Carlyle use a handkerchief. Only once he saw Carlyle use his fingers "which he did very adroitly without smearing them."

Even though in late years apart, the very years were a further bond and Carlyle could rightly commend himself "as now probably your oldest friend."

There was another oldest friend whom FitzGerald cherished. That old friend, Alfred Tennyson, came also to visit him at Woodbridge. It was at Little Grange, near the end of FitzGerald's life. Their friendship was of long standing. It was, on FitzGerald's part, a friendship of love and jealousy. The early Tennyson, the Tennyson of pre-"In Memoriam" days, was a favorite poet of his; the later poet irritated him. Frequently Tennyson's poems infuriated FitzGerald, and in that fury one feels less anger than an unconscious acknowledgment of what he himself was missing and on what he had turned his back. Yet never for a moment did he doubt Alfred's genius. In one of his desperate moments over the fate of England FitzGerald said that if he had had Tennyson's voice, he would not have mumbled for years over "In Memoriam" and "The Princess," but sung such strains as would have revived the Spartan Men to guard the territory they had won.

The voice he admired, but not the new works, which he annotated unflatteringly: "I can't," he informed Wright in February 1875, "read him out of the new Editions & altogether think he had better shut up after 1842. But he *said* & I dare say *says* things to be remembered: decisive Verdicts: which I hope some one makes note of—post memoranda . . ."

Like a busy but annoyed bee he continued to annotate his friend's poems; and then, as it not infrequently happened to him, remorse set in. He told Wright:

I have had some remorse about that annotated Tennyson passing into other hands before my own Death—or his. Not that I want it any more; on the contrary was glad to hand over to you, as a much younger man with equal reverence for A.T. But I know his sensitiveness on the matter; & if he heard that even your Master had seen it, he would be distressed & would not be persuaded but that others would see it also; that it would get into Print etc. I believe I ought to have left it sealed up to be delivered to you "post mortem." Do you understand this? . . .

The annotated Tennyson is in Trinity Library and it might sadden Tennyson to know that nobody is in a rush to see the annotations in print. If there was malice in FitzGerald, the Laureate did not lag behind, either. He dedicated *Tiresias* to his Old Fitz—a friendly gesture:

> *Old Fitz, who from your suburb grange*
> *Where once I tarried for a while,*
> *Glance at the wheeling Orb of change,*
> *And greet it with a kindly smile;*

That was the last thing FitzGerald would do. Tennyson knew that only too well. After describing FitzGerald with doves flitting about him, he gave full praise to the Rubáiyát. His son Hallam had found some old manuscripts and those Tennyson offered to:

> *My Fitz, and welcome as I know*
> *Less for its own than for the sake*
> *Of one recalling gracious times,*
> *When in our younger London days,*
> *You found some merit in my rhymes,*
> *And I more pleasure in your praise.*

A certain condescending cattiness can here be felt. Anyway, by the time *Tiresias* was in print, FitzGerald was in his grave.

Tennyson's visit to Woodbridge was an occasion of happiness for both of them. One is usually frightened when chroniclers of bygone days ask one to try to imagine a certain incident. Yet there must be exceptions, and the September morning with the blue sky above the Deben is as good as any. A train pulls into Woodbridge station, which is less than a stone's throw from the Deben. From the train alight two distinguished figures. The one with a beard is the Laureate himself; the other, looking up with adoration, is Hallam, father's biographer-to-be. All the way from London the Laureate has spoken of the gracious days which he had spent with Old Fitz's praise. Hallam listened respectfully, endeavoring to memorize his father's words.

Under the blue sky they walk briskly to the Cross Roads where, as befits his dignity and mellifluous voice, the Laureate does not allow the traffic oozing from four directions to hinder his progress. They stop a stranger from whom they inquire where Mr. FitzGerald lives. The stranger replies that indeed he knows that gentleman's residence. Guided by him, they reach Seckford Street and Mr. FitzGerald's home. Mr. FitzGerald turns out to be the Woodbridge police inspector. What Tennyson thought of Woodbridge's illiteracy is not part of the picture. After a while they find somebody who has heard of the other, less important, Mr. Fitz-Gerald and they are directed to Little Grange.

Tennyson sent in his card. "Dear old Fitz," he wrote on it, "I am passing through and am here." The card was handed to the housekeeper, who took it to FitzGerald: after twenty years the old friends met again. Of the visit Hallam said:

In September 1876 my father and I visited FitzGerald at Woodbridge. He was affectionate, genial and humourous, declaring that the captain of his lugger was one of the greatest of men. The views that Fitz expressed to me on literature were original and interesting, but the old man never got off his own platform to look at the work of modern authors. He had always wanted men like Thackeray and my father to go along with his crotchets, which were many. He had not been carried away by their genius out of himself and out of his own old Cambridge critical grove; and had not like them grown with the times. . . .My father was charmed with the picture of the lonely philosopher a "man of humorous-melancholy mark," with his grey floating locks, sitting among his doves, which perched about him on the head and shoulder and knee, and cooed to him as he sat in the sunshine, beneath the roses.

FitzGerald, who after having been mother-ridden and sister-ridden had now become niece-ridden, put them up at The Bull. After the Tennysons' departure another bit of Woodbridge illiteracy took place. The innkeeper asked FitzGerald who the guests had been, and when told, declared he had never heard of the Laureate.

FitzGerald would willingly have ended his life in the lodgings above the shop in Market Hill, and had his landlord not married again he would have stayed there for good; but the new wife thought it common to have a lodger, so he had to go. For the first time in his life he went to live in his own house: Little Grange. Since the nearest bell rings loudest, old age seems to rise out of all proportion. But with him it was true enough. At twenty-five he was already middle-aged, and after his short and sharp marriage, old age set in. His old age however was only one of manners and crotchets; with people and things he liked he remained touchingly young till the end, and now into his young heart there came Posh.

Those who pretend to have a sort of knowledge of FitzGerald snigger when the name of Posh is mentioned. There is, they believe, something ridiculous and naughty about the relationship between the well-to-do literary man and the simple fisherman. They think it riotously funny, and their faces light up as if they had heard an off-color joke which amused them. Yet there is nothing funny about it, for it did neither of them any good. FitzGerald put the surprised Posh on a pedestal, and when poor uncomfortable Posh stepped off the pedestal there was no stopping him till he reached the workhouse where he died.

The Posh business is a sad example of FitzGerald's lack of knowledge of men. If the critics who maintain that he turned to translations because he had little imagination are right in their contention, then Posh should be their shining proof. FitzGerald ruined Posh by attributing qualities to him which he not only did not possess but had never heard of. FitzGerald's love could not destroy Thackeray, for he was FitzGerald's match; Browne, as often happens to gentle men, went his own quiet way; but Posh, the simple Suffolk sailor, received the whole impact of that tempest which with FitzGerald was love.

It is almost unfair to give without asking anything in return. That was what ruined Posh. It is true that FitzGerald wanted in return the qualities with which in his imagination he had endowed Posh; but unaware of all that, Posh thought that his guvernor was a rum 'un, and therefore drank more than was good for him. The lot of seamen and fishermen is not easy: the sea is grim, the wind is hard, and life itself is grim and hard. If then there suddenly comes a rich gentleman with a plaid shawl round his shoulder, a top hat on his head, and friends tap their foreheads when he goes by, one becomes suspicious and stubborn too. The more the gentleman gives, the more canny one has to be. The rule, one knows, is that one has to work hard for everything; if everything is showered on one, suspicion grows and stubbornly one goes one's own way; for one's independence seems to be threatened. Resistance is instinctive. Often I had motored to Aldborough, to Lowestoft, to Dunwich, to Southwold, and as far as Great Yarmouth. I had watched the trawlers, talked to the men, and on all those trips Posh was in my mind. Men of his ilk are fond of money, but they know it is not found on the pavement, and even if it were on the pavement they would have to pick it up themselves. Their outlook is limited by the sea, the pubs, and their families. The toffs are so completely outside their orbits that, for them, they do not exist.

At Orford and Aldborough I went duck shooting, with men of Posh's kind taking me out in their boats. One cold November evening I had gone out with one like him. We went to a small island and waited for the duck that were feeding far out to come inland. There was a little moon wafted on wind and, in the distance, like a huge half-circle, were the sounds of the curlew.

While we waited I talked to my companion. We spoke of the weather, the duck, his boat, and the wind, and somehow or other, when the conversation drifted away from his subjects, it simply died; for nothing outside his world was of interest to him, and the comings and goings of people inland brought no spark of recognition from him. So we spoke of duck again and he told me how much they paid him in Aldborough for duck. I said it would be more profitable to sell them at Woodbridge or Ipswich where they fetched a fairer price. It was as though I told someone in Doncaster that, if he wished to sun himself, he should do it preferably in Bali.

That evening when we parted I thought again of Posh into whose grim life, unasked, had come the son of Mary Frances. Poor bewildered Posh, I said, and I had to add: poor bewildered FitzGerald; but he at least could afford his bewilderment.

On Browne's premature death [says Havelock Ellis] Fitz-Gerald's heart was empty. In 1859 at Lowestoft FitzGerald as he wrote to Mrs. Browne, "used to wander about the shore at night longing for some fellow to accept me who might give some promise of filling up a very vacant place in my heart." It was then that he met Posh (Joseph Fletcher) a fisherman, 6 feet tall, said to be of the best Suffolk type, both in body and character. Posh reminded FitzGerald of his dead friend Browne; he made him captain of his lugger and was thereafter devoted to him. Posh was, said Fitz-Gerald, "a man of the finest Saxon type, with a complexion vif, male et flamboyant, blue eyes, a nose less than Roman, more than Greek and strictly auburn hair that any woman could envy." Further he was a man of simplicity of soul, justice of thought, tenderness of nature, a gentleman of Nature's grandest type, "in fact the greatest man" FitzGerald had ever met. Posh was not, however, quite so absolutely perfect as this description.

Havelock Ellis's summing up is fairly accurate. The impact of FitzGerald's love would have been frightening to anybody less simple than Posh. It was no fault of Posh that in him FitzGerald thought to have found everything he did not possess and yet everything he admired. The sea had always been FitzGerald's friend; but if one lives in Suffolk one takes easily to the sea. It is always there and the air has salt in it. FitzGerald was not a sailor in the technical sense. When he was on board his boat, he mostly read or looked at the sea or the land. Strictly speaking, he was no yachtsman. As Browne for him had been the perfect horseman, so now Posh was the complete sailor. For FitzGerald, who had fought with the intricacies of Persian and Spanish, the man who fought the sea was a demigod.

In another letter, a copy of which Mr. Paine gave me, FitzGerald wrote thus of Posh to Woolner on March 8, 1867:

. . . The Sailor I now speak of is a moving Statue of Strength and Pliancy too; like one of the Elgin Marbles;

[two words illegible] in a Gurnsey which is a fine Dress for a fine Figure. When he has sat in the Cabin with the Light coming down, I have been reminded of the grand Figure on the Top of M. Angelo's Medici Tomb, the Cast of which is in the Crystal Palace, especially when the Organ plays without—is the finest Sight to me now of all the London Sights. And this man has a large simple Soul and Dignity of Manner, all of a piece; much more the *Gentleman* than the Gentlefolks of the Place he belongs to: & very much more Ladylike than the Ladies.

It stands to reason that if one endows a human being with such qualities, trouble and disappointment follow.

FitzGerald, as he afterwards told Posh, had spotted him some time before he made his acquaintance. In the evenings in Lowestoft, having arrived there in his ship the *Scandal,* he would walk about on the seashore with his heart empty but with a full bottle of rum in his pocket for anyone who would pick him up and talk to him. Thus he saw Posh for the first time. At that period Posh was the owner of a beach lugger. Fish were still plentiful, and Posh made a good living. In the spring of 1866 FitzGerald came to stay at Lowestoft in order to be near him. In the daytime they were out in the punt, in the evenings they drank, smoked, and talked at the Suffolk Restaurant, or went to Posh's home, for he had a wife and children. According to Posh, FitzGerald usually went to sea in a silk hat and wore a woman's boa round his neck. That year Posh gave up his punt and bought an old lugger, the *William Tell*. He borrowed fifty pounds from FitzGerald and fifty pounds from Newsom, the skipper of the *Scandal*. Newsom wanted no security for his loan, but FitzGerald did. "Remember your debts," he said to Posh, "remember your debts."

Now it is curious that a man as generous and un-mercenary as FitzGerald, the very man who filled Posh with ambition, should from the outset have bickered with him about money. FitzGerald had always been more ready to give than to take, but with Posh it was a different matter. He would urge Posh to better his position, give him money for that purpose, and then start being unpleasant about it. It was akin to frustration to be aware that sturdy, independent Posh could not be completely dominated with money. "The other day," FitzGerald would write to him, "an old Friend sent me £10 which was one half of what he said he had borrowed of me *thirty years ago!* I told him that, on my honour, I wholly forgot ever having lent him any money. I could only remember once *refusing* to lend him some. So here is *one* man who remembered his Debts better than his Creditor did."

Posh was not moved by such exhortations. He was not a good debtor, and what annoyed FitzGerald was that he would not keep his accounts properly. The cook who knows that her master's eyes follow her figure with more interest than her cooking will cease to be a keen cook; thus a debtor, and later a partner, will not be so scrupulous when he has been given to understand that he is the greatest man in the world.

After the *William Tell* came the *Meum and Tuum*, the lugger FitzGerald had built at Lowestoft for Posh; and they went into partnership as herring merchants.

The man of inaction delighted in being a herring merchant. It brought him, he thought, nearer to Posh, and there was something exquisite in being a herring merchant after having done the Rubáiyát and spent most of his time among books. For Posh, on the other hand, to be a herring merchant was a grim reality; consequently the *Meum and Tuum* did not become the bridge, as FitzGerald hoped, between his heart and that of Posh. Posh drank hard and in the evenings was half-drunk. The life of a fisherman is full of vexation; ashore, he relaxes with beer and more beer. At least so it was with Posh. And as it had been with Browne, so also it was with Posh: FitzGerald would love, be hurt, lose his temper, despise himself for it, exhort, and then lose his temper again. That sort of loving bullying does not please Suffolk men. Under it they go their own way, and, notwithstanding his affection for his rum old guvernor, Posh went his, which consisted mainly of not keeping accounts and of getting drunk. It was perhaps the only time in FitzGerald's life that he pitted his will against another's and was, in the end, the loser——though Posh lost more than he.

"I believe," said FitzGerald, "I have smoked my pipe every evening but one with Posh at his house, which his quiet little Wife keeps tidy and pleasant. . . . I have told him he is liable to one Danger (the Hare with many friends)——so many wanting him *to drink*."

FitzGerald advised him to take, if he must, gin and water but not beer. Posh continued to drink beer. The herring merchants did not prosper, yet in the beginning it was all roses if not fish. FitzGerald would say to Posh: "Oh dear, oh dear, Poshy. Two F's in the firm, Fitz-Gerald and Fletcher, herring salesmen——when Poshy catches any, which isn't as often as it might be, you know, Poshy!"

Posh was fond of him, too. He was kind, had a sense of fun, and, if only FitzGerald had left him alone with his beer and no accounts, everything might have turned out to be splendid. As FitzGerald had enjoyed the company of Mrs. Browne and her children, so he was moved by the quiet family life of Posh. Both are wistful pictures of a man who had gone through life quite unaware of why he himself would never have his own family circle.

In September 1872, FitzGerald was again at Lowestoft. Six years had gone by since he had fallen under the spell of Posh. That spell had now gone. It was impossible to continue believing in Posh, and Posh was no longer keen to be believed in. He drank more than ever; the herring business proved to be unlucrative; when there was money, Posh drove about in a gig and did not heed FitzGerald's advice. FitzGerald saw the pedestal cracking.

It is said that age mellows one, but that generalization is often fallacious. A younger FitzGerald might have put up longer with Posh; the man over sixty could not. Moreover, Posh simply refused to listen. The financial side was of some importance, but it was the disillusioned heart which brought the friendship to an end. Symbols and idols are not easy to deal with, especially when the symbol of the sea turns out to be rather the symbol of beer, and the idol is not altogether accurate about tackle and such things. Posh did not want to do FitzGerald; with his easy-going nature he was as ready to do himself, too. But the adulation had gone to his head, and he resented a love he could not understand. He was grown up, he had a beard, he needed soulful counsel from no one.

Thus, in 1872, Poshy had become Joseph Fletcher again. He had caught no fish and had come home with nearly all his boat's fleet of nets torn to bits in the previous week's wind. Nevertheless, FitzGerald still tried. In order to keep Posh's mind off the beer bottle, he took him to *The Merchant of Venice* where, as said before,

Posh fell asleep. But on the last day of the year poor Posh had become completely Joseph Fletcher: "Joseph Fletcher," FitzGerald wrote, "As you cannot talk to me without confusion, I wrote a few words to you on the subject of the two grievances you began about this morning."

The first grievance was that Posh thought FitzGerald wanted him to work under his, Posh's, father, whereas all FitzGerald had said to him was that he should have his father as partner in order to take the more steady man's advice. Of course, putting it even that way, Posh would have none of it. The second grievance was that FitzGerald wished to take out a bill-of-sale on tackle and ship. He would not take advantage of it but use it only as a protection for Posh from his other creditors. "If you cannot," ended up FitzGerald, "see all this on reflection, there is no use my talking or writing more about it." Needless to say, Posh did not see FitzGerald's point of view; in fact he never did.

In January 1874, FitzGerald had to admit that Fletcher had given up seeing him, though once he had come to the house when he was out. Had he taken some desperate step? FitzGerald hoped for his family's sake that he had not. Undoubtedly the loving heart was cooling fast. Yet he still admitted that Fletcher had some greatness, albeit wanting in conscience. They must, all the same, part; and here again it should be emphasized how little FitzGerald considered another person's background, his own set habits, and well-filled purse. It was lack of imagination and falling short in understanding which had turned him against Posh. Nonetheless, he made a last effort to persuade Posh to mend his ways and lead the life he, FitzGerald, considered the best for him. Posh was adamant and, in June, FitzGerald cried out in a sad voice: "I am advertized in the *Gazette* as being no longer a Fishmonger and my last Hand is played."

And in a sad voice, too, in his old age, in the workhouse Posh could say: "He would have given me a gold mine."

So, then, ended the tale of his last great love, and now all there was left for him was old age, ducks on the pond, nieces, his books, and his *Readings from Crabbe*. It is interesting that fundamentally Posh had had no influence on him. Browne, at least, had inspired *Euphranor*, but Posh was no inspiration. FitzGerald had started collecting Suffolk sea words and phrases long before Posh entered his life. The answer probably is that Posh was, in FitzGerald's eyes, a complete masterpiece, needing no translation into words. Furthermore, it might be that just because Posh was so human, FitzGerald's creative talent received no spark from him. Had he read of Posh, it might have been a different matter, especially if Posh had lived a long time before.

FitzGerald's old age was comparatively pleasant. True, his eyesight had begun seriously to fail; true, his friends were dying, but he had seen most of them so seldom that he could think of them as well dead as alive. The world left him alone. There were people in London who thought the Rubáiyát was the greatest work of the age, but Woodbridge was far from London.

C. S. Keane has left us two pictures of him: "At Dunwich," he wrote to Alexander Macdonald, "there was an old literate who had the only lodging in the place, a great friend of Tennyson's and of poor Thackeray's and quite a character—an Irishman, an author and bookworm, and who remembers Kean and the Kembles and Liston, and full of talk about old times and 'dead and gone people.' . . ."

The following year, when he had come to know Fitz-Gerald better, he wrote of him again to Macdonald:

. . . I was staying in Suffolk with a bookish old scholar, one of the old school—friend of Carlyle's and Tennyson and Thackeray, and we talked art and the belles lettres all day in his garden, and smoked long churchwarden pipes in the evening. I find he is a great unknown poet in certain literary circles in town—I mean the Rossetti set—and that a certain translation that he made of some Persian poems, and published anonymously, and another work—translations of Calderon's plays—are considered by them as the greatest works of the age.

FitzGerald sitting in his garden, FitzGerald with doves alighting on his shoulder, are pleasing sights. He had at last found his true milieu, namely the peace of the old. His many crotchets and even his rudeness were but the line of defense of his peace. His sense of humor remained with him, but his heart was already at rest. The last flame that had been Posh had died, and now there were the ducks quacking on the pond and the quiet of the tree's shadow. His had been a long life from which he had taken little, though what he had taken he enjoyed. Dubbed a hermit and an eccentric, he nevertheless stayed in the harness he had made for himself till the end. His dislike for contemporary writers was with him till the end, too. Of George Eliot, for instance, he said: "All the Magazines have some one Article or two more readable to me than George Eliot upon whom I was being thrown in despair." But of Crabbe, dear old Crabbe, dead for such a long time, he could joyfully exclaim: "Here—I am back at my old Desk—with positively—my old Crabbe!"

So he was in his old age. I have been told by those who knew him—who are now themselves as old as he was when he died—that at times he walked down the streets of Woodbridge barefooted, having, so they imagined, forgotten his shoes. That is a nice little tidbit for his legend, but as he suffered from bronchial trouble, it is quite unlikely that his housekeeper let him go abroad unshodden. His friends still visited with him, and he went to stay with nieces, or with George Crabbe, the Third, who was vicar at Merton in Norfolk; or to London to see Fanny Kemble, after endless years; or to stand outside Carlyle's house in Cheyne Row, which he had not seen for five-and-twenty years, and there the notice "To Let" drove him almost tearfully away.

In May 1879 his brother John died at Boulge Hall. To go to Boulge from Little Grange is simple enough. One goes out of the house, turns to the right, at Melton Hill turns to the left, and walks straight down the road which leads past Foxborough to Bredfield Pump and then to Boulge. It is roughly two-and-a-half miles. Yet FitzGerald did not go. In 1879 the convention of being present at a family funeral was as strong as the Royal Navy; and one can well picture Woodbridge buzzing with the dreadful tale: Mr. FitzGerald of Little Grange had not attended the funeral of Mr. FitzGerald of Boulge Hall; and brothers, too, they were.

Yet FitzGerald had not been uninterested in his brother's illness. He reported to Wright as far back as March that his brother had had a bladder attack which had confined him to bed for the last month. Their father had suffered from something of the same. He thought his brother would not recover from the attack; and he, himself, felt that his own end would come in a similar manner, "before the Heart can polish one off decently." On May 7 he wrote again to Wright, saying his brother had died peacefully. He had not suffered and lay much dozing. He wished himself a similar end, and then, after the funeral, he wrote to Wright as follows: "My brother was buried yesterday—I suppose I ought to feel ashamed that I did not go. I should have done so had there not been Kerriches & DeSoyers to represent me & more than me."

It is easy, if one feels in the mood for it, to explain motives of others, quite forgetful of the fact that motives are often so obscure and at times so simple that they can be overlooked. It is possible that FitzGerald did not go to his brother's funeral for reasons even psychiatrists might find rather complicated; it is also possible that he did not go because he lost his temper with the collar he was trying to button for the occasion. It does not truly matter what the motive was, but what stands out is that he could decide not to go without taking the slightest notice of the stern convention of his time.

Four years later his own end came. It came in June. Of that June he said to Fanny Kemble, "and with June come my two Nieces from Lowestoft: & then the

Longest Day will come; & we shall begin declining towards Winter again, after so shortly escaping from it." But there would be no more winter for him. He was seventy-four, still vigorous, his mind still keen; nevertheless the coming winter was simply not for him. . . .

And thinking thus of FitzGerald, I turned to my wife and asked her to find me his last letter, for any minute now the man would die on me. It is, I must confess, a sad occasion to lose a man who has been in one's thought for two years. With him I rose in the morning, and of him I thought before I fell asleep. In that last letter speaking of a friend's death he quoted these words of Madame de Sévigné: *"Voilà ma petite protestation respecteuse à la Providence."* The night of June 13, 1883, is my own respectful protestation, for that night was the end of him.

He died at Merton, in the house of Crabbe, whom he had known as a child in Bredfield. He had been in good spirits in the evening, going to bed around ten. At a quarter to eight in the morning Crabbe knocked on the door and, getting no answer, went in and found him as though sleeping peacefully but quite dead.

Once one is dead and gone, there is little more to be said. There is that terrible thing about the dead, that they *are* dead. You can turn them, prod them, cry over them, pray for them, yet they remain dead. Even for me, who lived with him in the old room, the cord is broken, the contact gone, and the silence of the grave is all that is left of the man I have known. For that reason I must go back to him and his thoughts before death had lost him for good. So I hold hard to the words he wrote sixteen days before his death to a niece about the fatal illness of a mutual friend: "It seems strange to me to be so seemingly alert—certainly alive—amid such fatalities with younger and stronger people. But even while I say so, the hair may break, and the suspended sword fall."

Whether one has the grace of Faith or the complacency of the unbeliever, one has to part from the dead. FitzGerald was taken to his grave in Boulge churchyard, and the rooks and the trees and the peaceful meadow were around him. Among the mourners were Archdeacon Groome, Professor Cowell, Aldis Wright, Alfred Smith, and Mowbray Donne. The Rector, the Rev. F. Joplin, conducted the service. On one side of the grave, on which I have sat so often, is this inscription: "Edward FitzGerald Born 31 March 1809 Died 14 June 1883." On the other side: "It Is He That Hath Made Us And Not We Ourselves"—which is from Psalm c, 3. And the *Suffolk Chronicle* gave this obituary notice:

The sudden death is announced of Mr. Edward FitzGerald of the Little Grange while on a visit to the Rev. G. Crabbe at Merton, Norfolk. Mr. FitzGerald retired to rest on

Wednesday night in his usual health and not coming down to breakfast the next morning Mr. Crabbe went to his room and found him lying dead in bed. The cause of death is supposed to be disease of the heart. The deceased gentleman was about 75 years of age. He was the younger brother of Mr. John Purcell-FitzGerald of Boulge Hall. He was of a particularly retiring disposition and, inheriting a handsome fortune, he was able to devote himself to the literary pursuits he loved so well. Mr. FitzGerald married the daughter of Bernard Barton the Quaker Poet but soon after they separated by mutual consent though they remained on completely friendly terms. Mr. FitzGerald's literary works were mostly printed for private circulation. Formerly he was very fond of yachting and his pretty little schooner the *Scandal* was some years ago well known on the waters of the Deben.

When a man dies, one likes, if one is not as gifted as journalists on the *Suffolk Chronicle,* to look at what he has left behind. First of all, FitzGerald left behind Cowell and Wright, who, by the sheer weight of their years, talked themselves into the twentieth century. These two went for walks, as old men do, and spoke of FitzGerald, and of who would have believed it that the Rubáiyát should have become so famous; and indeed would not Old Fitz, who at heart had always been a Christian gentleman, be surprised if he knew of the philosophies and theories people were attaching to his work. And Aldis Wright watched over the reputation of his dead friend. The trial of Oscar Wilde was still burning in people's memories. Literary heroes ought to be as simple and guileless as people pretend they themselves are. The marriage with Lucy Barton had not been an edifying incident, and the whole Posh business could be completely misinterpreted. So Wright watched over FitzGerald, quite unaware that old Posh would sell, here and there, one of his guvernor's letters when thirst drove him to it. Thus, then, watched Wright, and he was surely pleased with the biographers who side-stepped the issue and dared only to call FitzGerald effeminate, which he was not.

Besides the two men at Cambridge, he left behind many good friends, one of whom, John Allen, could say: "I owe very much to my dear friend. I daily strive to act on lessons that were brought to my conscience by what I saw in him—a most true friend."

He also left behind a lot of silly people; but that one invariably does. The silly people thought they had found their own excuse in the Rubáiyát, and arty-crafty little parchment-bound copies would lie on their tables and be dipped into by them, thinking they had found their importance.

He also inspired some excruciatingly bad jingles, one of which is enough to quote. A laudatory poem attached to one of the American editions contained these two lines:

We'll love with love that knows no change
The Hermit-bard of Little Grange.

He was given a memorial tablet in Cambridge. Bernard Shaw was asked to inaugurate it, but declined on the grounds that he was no Fitz fan, which, on afterthought, is rather explainable. During the ceremony the only literary figure in sight was Sir Arthur Quiller-Couch, but he hurried on, taking no interest. On the other hand, the Iranian Minister was present.

But of course there were more tangible things Fitz-Gerald left behind: Mr. W. Arnott, the Woodbridge auctioneer, sold all his worldly possessions at Little Grange. In the sale catalogue FitzGerald was referred to as a scholar and philosopher. Sale catalogues make impersonal reading. Even the owner often does not recognize his own property. There is, moreover, much of a muchness about catalogues and contents.

In FitzGerald's kitchen there were such utensils as strainer, grater, baking tins, charcoal stove, two fire-baskets, cuckoo clock, coal scuttles, and kitchen fender; in the vestibule: a small barometer, iron folding chair, and bronze umbrella stand. Suddenly the sale items become more personal: folding picture-ladder; painted bookcase with wire doors, 78 inches long, 30 inches wide; and patent Minima organ in oak case— these he had truly possessed and not picked up either out of necessity or boredom. In the inner hall was a

294

stuffed heron in a glass case, a mahogany reading stand and small glass easel. He had something of his brother's love for clocks. In the inner hall were two clocks, two more in the study, bookcases in every room. Such items attract one's attention as: ladies' inlaid work box, sandwich case, toasting fork, and two pairs of scissors. His best pictures had been sent to Christie's; among those sold at Little Grange were a "Pair of Theatrical Mezzotints after Zoffany," "Portrait of Thackeray by Himself," and "Photograph of a Fisherman." That picture of Posh was bought by a Mr. Lewis.

His china was plentiful and included an elegant painted plate from the collection of W. M. Thackeray; also Wedgwood medallions of Wesley and Lord Nelson. Then there was a bust of Tennyson, bronze watch stand with armed figure and letter weight, and a statuette of Thackeray. But one still feels sad about the "Photograph of the Fisherman" which had fetched only five shillings.

The drawing room was well furnished and Fitz-Gerald had been fond of ormolu. The wine closet contained the following:

2 bottles brandy	4 sherry
2 ditto whisky	1 claret
3 pts Scotch ale	2 Vichy water
4 bottles & 2 pts port	

Among the pictures which went up at Christie's,

the highest price, namely 67 guineas, was paid for J. Van Der Capella's *River Scene*. There were pictures by David Teniers, Titian, Bassano, del Piombo, Cuyp, and Romney.

The library was sold at Little Grange, too. There were 147 lots of books and, curiously enough, all they tell is that the library had been the library of a gentleman with good literary taste and of catholic reading. A few items should suffice: *The Suffolk Stud Book,* Piozzi's *Travels,* Ayscough's *Index to Shakespeare,* Blackie's *Imperial Gazeteer, Dictionaire d' Histoire et Geographie, Clarissa* (7 vols.), Middleton's *Cicero,* three lots of Mme. de Sévigné's *Letters,* and *Great Crime of 1860.*

It seems to me that among his worldly possessions perhaps the wine closet, the three lots of Mme. de Sévigné's *Letters,* and the photograph of the fisherman bring him back most vividly.

By the time I had, so to speak, put FitzGerald into his grave, it was time to say good-by to it. My last days at Boulge were of excessive heat. The stream which fed the pond, now bereft of duck but with water hens returning in strength, had ceased flowing. The grass was burnt and yellow, and if I heard a pheasant calling it called neither for my gun nor for me. The house itself, waiting for the removers to take away my books, pictures, and furniture, was silent. And I recalled that, when I had come to live at Boulge, I had believed I might stay there all my life. Because I believe in eternity, I mixed it up with permanency. That last day I knew that if I had my way I should have a house, furnish it from top to bottom, lay out the garden, find a quiet corner for my tomb, and then leave.

So, on that last hot morning, I went to say good-by to FitzGerald's grave, and at his grave I asked myself whether I had brought him back to life as he had appeared to me when I saw him in the old room. One things was certain—I had not tried to make any cap fit. I had no preconceived ideas about him and he could only blame himself if I had come to like and admire him. I had wandered round the old room without prejudice. I had not taken to his mother, though I respected her for the woman of iron will she was. I turned on Bernard Barton, but toward the end nearly relented. About Lucy I had no emotions except pity for the man she married. Thackeray, because of their friendship, became a dear, often pathetic figure; Browne, gentle, handsome, and kind; and for Posh I was sorry as I was sorry for FitzGerald, too. But for me, above them all, towered FitzGerald himself, whose age had let him lead his own life, and because it had let him, he repaid it with the Rubáiyát, the *Letters,* and the fine friendship he dispensed.

Then, before I had time to say good-by, I was called back: the removal vans had arrived. Shortly after, my car, having left the Hall, passed the Cottage; soon it would pass Bredfield House and Farlingay Hall, but not Little Grange.

As the car came out of the Park and the road turned toward Pump Corner, I heard, as it were, a faint click: it was the door of the old room which had closed.

Boulge Hall, Woodbridge, April 1946.
Kyrenia, Cyprus, May 1948.

From *Copinger's Manors of Suffolk*, Vol. VII

THE FAMILY OF FITZGERALD

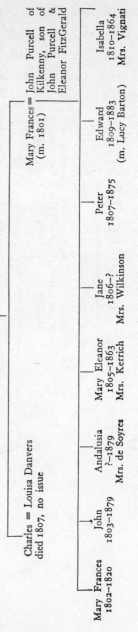

John FitzGerald (died 1818), = Mary FitzGerald, daughter of
son of John FitzGerald of | Keane FitzGerald of Tot-
Williamstown, Co. Waterford | teridge, Herts

Mary Frances = John Purcell of
(m. 1801) Kilkenny, son of
John Purcell &
Eleanor FitzGerald

Mary Frances 1802–1820

John 1803–1879

Andalusia ?–1879 Mrs. de Soyres

Charles = Louisa Danvers died 1807, no issue

Mary Eleanor 1805–1863 Mrs. Kerrich

Jane 1806–? Mrs. Wilkinson

Peter 1807–1875

Edward 1809–1883 (m. Lucy Barton)

Isabella 1810–1864 Mrs. Vignati

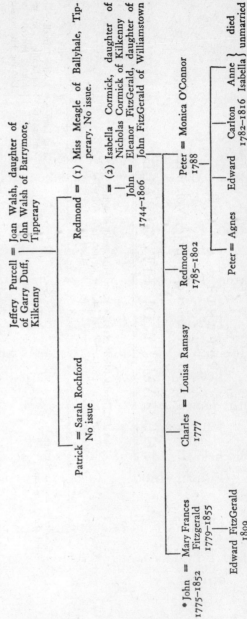

From the *Farnbam Manuscripts*, Vol. VI, Part 2, 1st Series

THE FAMILY OF PURCELL

BARONS OF LOUGHMOE

Jeffery Purcell of Garry Duff, Kilkenny = Joan Walsh, daughter of John Walsh of Barrymore, Tipperary

Patrick = Sarah Rochford — No issue

Redmond = (1) Miss Meagle of Ballyhale, Tipperary. No issue.

= (2) Isabella Cormick, daughter of Nicholas Cormick of Kilkenny

John 1744–1806 = Eleanor FitzGerald, daughter of John FitzGerald of Williamstown

Charles 1777 = Louisa Ramsay

Redmond 1785–1802

Peter 1788 = Monica O'Connor

John 1775–1852 = Mary Frances Fitzgerald 1779–1855

Edward FitzGerald 1809

Peter = Agnes

Carlton   Anne 1782–1816   Edward   Isabella } died unmarried

* Since John Purcell changed his name to FitzGerald, I have put the eight children into the FitzGerald Table.—M. de P.

Bibliography

Allen, E. Heron. *Some Sidelights upon the Rubáiyát of Omar Khayyám.* London: H. S. Nichols, 1898.

Barton, F. B. (ed.). *Some New Letters of Edward FitzGerald.* London: Williams & Norgate, 1923.

Barton, Lucy (ed.). *Selections from the Poems and Letters of Bernard Barton.* Memoir by Edward FitzGerald. Hall Virtue, 1849.

Benson, A. C. *Edward FitzGerald.* "English Men of Letters" Series. London: Macmillan, 1905.

Byth, James. *Edward FitzGerald and Posh.* London: John Long, 1908.

Brookfield, F. M. *The Cambridge Apostles.* London: Pitman, 1906.

Browne, E. G. *A Literary History of Persia.* 2 vols. London: T. Fisher-Unwin, 1902–1906.

Clodd, Edward. *Memories.* London: Chapman & Hall, 1916.

Copper E. R. *A Suffolk Coast Garland*. London: Heath Cranton, 1928.

Cowell, George. *Life and Letters of Edward Byles Cowell*. London: Macmillan, 1904.

Driver, Leotas. *Fanny Kemble*. Chapel Hill: University of North Carolina Press, 1932.

Edward FitzGerald's Centenary Celebrations. A Souvenir. *East Anglian Daily Times,* 1909.

Edward FitzGerald's Letters to Bernard Quaritch. London: Bernard Quaritch, 1926.

FitzGerald, Edward (trans.). *The Rubáiyát of Omar Khayyám*. Commentary, H. M. Batson. Bibliographical Introduction, E. D. Ross. London: Methuen, 1900.

Gang, Charles (ed.). *A FitzGerald Medley*. London: Methuen, 1933.

Glyde, John. *The Life of Edward FitzGerald*. London: C. Arthur Pearson, 1900.

Groome, Francis Hyndes. *Two Suffolk Friends*. London: Blackwood, 1895.

Hannay, Neilson Campbell (ed.). *A FitzGerald Friendship. Letters to Bodham Donne*. With an Introduction and Notes in collaboration with

Mrs. Catherine Bodham Johnson. London: Faber & Faber, 1932.

Ince, R. *Calverley and Some Cambridge Wits.*

Johnson, Catharine B. (ed.). *W. B. Donne and His Friends.* London: Methuen, 1905.

Kemble, Frances Ann. *Records of a Girlhood.* 3 vols. London: R. Bentley, 1890.
————. *Records of Later Life.* London: R. Bentley, 1882.
————. *Further Records.* 2 vols. London: R. Bentley, 1890.

Layard, George. *Life and Letters of Charles Samuel Keene.* London: Sampson Lowe, 1892.

Lowestoft, Tymns. *East Anglian Notes and Queries.* 1869–70.

Lucas, E. V. *Bernard Barton and His Friends.* London: Edward V. Hicks, 1892.

MacLysaght, Edward. *Irish Life in the Seventeenth Century: After Cromwell.* Bradshaw Collection. Cambridge University Library.

Melville, Lewis. *William Makepeace Thackeray.* London: Benn, 1927.

Neff, Emery E. *O. Carlyle.* London: Allen & Unwin, 1932.

Nicolson, Harold. *Tennyson*. London: Constable, 1923.

Personal Remembrances of Sir W. Fredrick Pollock. 2 vols. London: Macmillan, 1887.

Prideaux, W. F. *Notes for a Bibliography of Edward FitzGerald*. London: Hollings, 1901.

Quaritch, Bernard. *Edward FitzGerald's Rubáiyát of Omar Khayyám*. London: Bernard Quaritch, 1899.

Ray, Gordon N. (ed.). *The Letters and Private Papers of W. M. Thackeray*. 4 vols. London: Oxford University Press, 1946–47.

Reid, T. Wemyss. *Life, Letters and Friendships of Richard Monckton Milnes, First Lord Houghton*. London: Cassell, 1891.

Ritchie, Hester Thackeray (ed.). *Letters of Anne Thackeray Ritchie*. London: Murray, 1924.

Schonfield, Hugh J. (ed.). *Letters to Frederick Tennyson*. London: Hogarth Press, 1930.

Tennyson, Hallam. *Alfred Lord Tennyson, a Memoir*. London: Macmillan, 1897.

———— (ed.). *Tennyson and His Friends*. London: Macmillan, 1911.

Tennyson, Julian. *Suffolk Scene*. London: Blackie & Son, 1939.

Terhune, Alfred McKinley. *The Life of Edward Fitz-Gerald, Translator of the Rubáiyát of Omar Khayyám.* Yale University Press and Oxford University Press, 1947.

Wright, Aldis (ed.). *The Works of Edward Fitz-Gerald, Letters and Literary Remains.* 7 vols. London: Macmillan, 1902.

Wright, Thomas. *The Life of Edward FitzGerald.* 2 vols. London: Grant Richards, 1904.

Young, G. M. *The Portrait of an Age.* Oxford University Press.

——— (ed.). *Early Victorian England.* Oxford University Press.